QUESTS FOR THE HISTORICAL JESUS

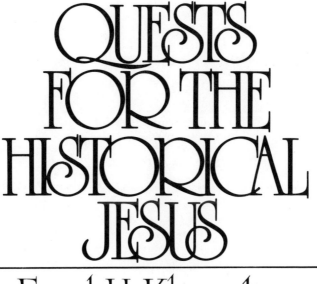

QUESTS FOR THE HISTORICAL JESUS

Fred H. Klooster

BAKER BIBLICAL MONOGRAPH

BAKER BOOK HOUSE
Grand Rapids, Michigan

Originally published as "Jesus Christ: History and Kerygma" in *Presbyterion: Covenant Seminary Review* 1 (1975): 23–50, 80–110. Reprinted here by permission.

PHOTOLITHOPRINTED BY CUSHING - MALLOY, INC.
ANN ARBOR, MICHIGAN, UNITED STATES OF AMERICA
1 9 7 7

To
the students
and faculties of

Covenant Theological Seminary
St. Louis, Missouri
General Assembly Presbyterian Seminary
Seoul, Korea
Korea Theological Seminary
Pusan, Korea
Reformed Theological Seminary
Kobe, Japan
Reformed Ministers' Institute
Taipei, Taiwan

Contents

Preface

The contents of this little work originated in a series of lectures presented in the spring of 1970 to the students and faculty of Covenant Theological Seminary, St. Louis, Missouri. I am grateful to the Covenant faculty for the invitation and for gracious hospitality on that occasion and subsequently. That invitation was the stimulus for my attempt to bring some clarity to my own understanding of the quests for the historical Jesus. These quests reflect the post-Enlightenment crisis in the relation of the Word of God and the Christ of that Word.

A lecture tour to the Orient during the spring of 1971 was initiated by the faculty of the General Assembly Presbyterian Seminary in Seoul, Korea. The encouragement and support of President J. H. Kromminga and the Board of Trustees of Calvin Theological Seminary made the visit to Korea possible. The interest and support of the Christian Reformed Board of World Missions enabled me to extend the lecture tour to Japan and Taiwan. The entire series of lectures was presented at the inviting institution in Seoul, at Korea Theological Seminary in Pusan, Korea, and at the Reformed Theological Seminary in Kobe, Japan. In a variety of abbreviations, the lectures were also presented in other institutions in Seoul and Taejon, Korea, and at a Reformed Ministers' Institute and the Evangelical Theological Seminary in Taipei, Taiwan. To the students and faculties of these many institutions, I am pleased to dedicate this book in thanks for warm hospitality shown me during these personally enriching visits.

In 1975 the first two issues of *Presbyterion: Covenant Seminary Review* contained the published version of these lectures. I am grateful to Baker Book House for making this material available to a wider public, and I express my thanks to Covenant Theological Seminary and the *Presbyterion* committee for permission to do so.

I hope this survey of the quests for the historical Jesus may help students and many others to recognize that the

Easter faith is firmly rooted in what the Son of God incarnate accomplished once-for-all through His historical life, death, and resurrection. "He was delivered over to death for our sins and was raised to life for our justification" (Rom. 4:25 NIV). We must confess in faith the authentic gospel truly rooted in history. "Beyond all question, the mystery of godliness is great:

> He appeared in a body,
>> was vindicated by the Spirit,
> was seen by angels,
>> was preached among the nations,
> was believed on in the world,
>> was taken up in glory."
>
> (I Tim. 3:16 NIV)

Chapter 1
The Old Quest
and Liberalism

When we Christians celebrate Good Friday and Easter, we celebrate events that really happened in the life of Jesus Christ our Lord. Do you recall the CBS television program called something like "Who, What, Where, When?"? The Christian can answer those questions emphatically because the Christian gospel is firmly rooted in history. Who? Jesus of Nazareth, the Son of God incarnate. What did he do? That takes a few more words, but the answer is historical. He was born of Mary; He lived, suffered, and died on Good Friday; and He rose again on Easter morning. Where? Places, cities, provinces, rivers, and lakes provide the concrete answer. When? Days and hours and dates—in the days of Caesar Augustus and Pontius Pilate. But, as we well know, not all the world's theologians present that view of the Christian faith. The relation of history and kerygma has become one of the great problems of theology. Myth, symbol, and saga have been invented to take the place of history in relation to the kerygma. Authentic Christianity, however, insists upon the historical basis of the Christian faith. That position has been under attack for a long time, and today these issues stand at the heart of theological debate. In this book I want to consider the basic question of the relation of history and kerygma.

Recent trends in theology, from H. S. Reimarus to Wolfhart Pannenberg—that is the scope of my subject. If Albert Schweitzer had a difficult task in surveying the developments from Reimarus to Wilhelm Wrede, think of the magnitude of my task. I shall deal first with the "Old Quest" for the historical Jesus in liberal theology. Then I want to consider Karl Barth and neo-orthodoxy in what I have called the "No Quest." After that my concern will be the "New Quest" of neo-liberalism. And finally, to retain the parallel, I shall review the "Now Quest" of Pannenberg.

As I begin to survey the Old Quest and liberalism, let me present a few of the slogans of the movement. The Old Quest began in 1778, and the movement flourished from roughly 1835 to 1900. The Old Quest ended in a historicism without the kerygma. The search for the historical Jesus led to a truncated history, and the Jesus of Scripture eluded their quest. From a theological perspective the Old Quest was ebionitic—it denied the deity of Jesus Christ. It pursued a Christology "from below," for it began and ended with the historical Jesus who was not believed to be God's Son incarnate. These are some of the characteristics of the Old Quest, and I will enlarge upon their meaning and significance in what follows.

The Old Quest was clearly a reaction to historical Christianity as it had been confessed in preceding centuries. The dogmas of the church were openly rejected, and they were usually rejected as the presupposition or starting point of the Old Quest. In those very presuppositions are already contained the conclusions at which the Old Quest arrived. The presuppositions of the Old Quest were those of the Enlightenment. Hence it was historic Christianity which was rejected, not just some of the ancient dogmas of the church. We must briefly review the pre-Enlightenment theology.

Pre-Enlightenment Theology

Christian theology prior to the Enlightenment involved a Christology "from above." The Son of God, second person of the Trinity, had become incarnate of the virgin Mary through the miraculous conception by the Holy Spirit. The supernatural activity of God in history was readily confessed. Indeed, all of history was understood to involve the activity of God. History was regarded as real history, but God was active in history. Pre-Enlightenment theology had no difficulty in acknowledging God's action in history. Of course such theology did not die with the Enlightenment, and, thank God, it will never die! Yet the attack upon it has been intense ever since the Enlightenment, and the attack continues unabated in our own day. While historic Christianity recognized the action of God in history, it did regard history as basic to the kerygma. Real events in history were basic to the Christian gospel—a real incarnation "in the fullness of time," a virgin birth from Mary at Bethlehem, the historical life of Jesus of Nazareth lived in Galilee and Judaea, crucifixion in Jerusalem on Friday, and resurrection from the tomb on the third day, and forty days later the ascension to heaven. Those historical events really happened! And the gospel is based on what Jesus Christ really did for our salvation.

As far as specific dogmas are concerned, these had been formulated by the Christian church through the following centuries in ecumenical councils. These dogmas do not represent the Christian faith as mere ideas divorced from history; on the contrary, the dogmas express a kerygma rooted in real history. These dogmas were rejected by the Old Quest in the name of historical objectivity and theology without presupposition (the Enlightenment myth). This rejection involved the decision of the first ecumenical council (held in Nicaea in 325) which confessed the true deity of Jesus Christ of Nazareth as *homoousios* with the Father. The subordinationistic view of Arius was thereby rejected at Nicaea. The decision of the second ecumenical council at Constantinople in 381 was also rejected by the Old Quest. There was a slight difference here, of course, since this council affirmed the full humanity of Jesus Christ over against a docetic tendency in the position of Apollinaris. The Old Quest was certainly interested in the full, historical humanity of Jesus. However, Constantinople in 381 affirmed the humanity of the Son of God incarnate. It confessed that Jesus was *vere deus, vere homo*. Hence the Old Quest also rejected the dogma of Constantinople. These dogmas were rejected as metaphysical categories reflecting the influence of the Greek spirit on the soil of the gospel, as Adolf von Harnack was to express it. Of course the decision at Chalcedon in 451 was especially objectionable to representatives of the Old Quest. This council confessed that Jesus Christ was *homoousios* with the Father as to His deity and *homoousios* with us as to His humanity. The conflict with Nestorius and Eutyches led Chalcedon to confess the mystery of one person in two natures—natures that were not fused or changed and not divided or separated. This decision was further safeguarded against the Monophysites in 553 and against the Monothelites in 680. One might add a reference to the satisfaction view of the atonement which was projected by Anselm and modified by the Reformers. However, this was never considered in ecumenical council.

The patristic church expressed itself ecumenically mainly on the doctrines of the Trinity and Christology.

Now it is this church dogma which the Old Quest rejected. This dogma was rejected because it was considered incompatible with the historical perspective of the Enlightenment. I wish to emphasize again that these dogmas of the early church from Nicaea through Chalcedon as well as the Reformation confessions do recognize real history as basic to the gospel, to the kerygma. The incarnation, the life-ministry of Jesus, the crucifixion, the resurrection—all of these were understood to be real events in history underlying the dogmas declared by the church. The dogma and confession of the church did not hang docetically in the air. It was dogma rooted in history. The church rejected Docetism as well as Ebionism, although those twin errors continued to threaten the church in a variety of ways. Jesus truly lived in Palestine during the years 1–30. He was crucified on a Friday under Pontius Pilate, and He rose again on the third day. That history was basic to the church's affirmation of the dogma concerning Jesus Christ. Kerygma and history were interlocked; the one was intimately related to the other. D. F. Strauss, a representative of the Old Quest, was correct when he stated that two things are presupposed in that position—that the Gospels contain history and that this history is supernatural history. This second presupposition was especially objectionable to the Old Quest, with its Enlightenment presuppositions.

This patristic dogma (Nicaea, Constantinople, Chalcedon) was accepted by the Roman Catholic church as well as the Greek Orthodox church (with differences regarding the *filioque*). And it was continued in the Reformation by both Lutherans and Calvinists. But this patristic dogma was already opposed by the ebionites as well as the docetists, by the Arians as well as the Abelardians. The Socinians of the Reformation period called it into question with their unitarianism and subordinationism. Even the Arminians, who claimed to hold the main lines of traditional dogma on the Trinity and Christology, also tended to weaken these dogmas along Socinian ways. The major changes, however—and that is the subject of this chapter—came with the rise of liberalism and the development of the Old Quest for the historical Jesus. It is noteworthy, but in no way praise-worthy, that this development took place largely within Protestantism itself.

Protestant scholasticism, a late-sixteenth- and seventeenth-century development, did indeed bring in some different emphases as a result of its synthesis with Cartesian rationalism. This scholastic tendency within Protestantism tended toward a one-sided intellectualism which did not do justice to the historical basis of the Christian faith. Evidence supports the contention that prior to the Enlightenment the significance of history for the kerygma was denied or neglected. But whatever warrant there was for reaction to the minimizing of history in Protestant scholasticism, the real impetus for the Old Quest came from the new presuppositions of the Enlightenment. This judgment is also expressed by Joachim Jeremias in his booklet *The Problem of the Historical Jesus:*

> To anyone who is not aware of the controversy, the question whether the historical Jesus and his message have any significance for the Christian faith must sound absurd. No one in the ancient church, no one in the church of the Reformation period and the two succeeding centuries thought of asking such a question. How is it possible that today this question is being asked in all seriousness, that it even occupies a central place in New Testament debate, and that in many quarters it is being answered with a decisive negative? For a widely held theological position maintains that the historical Jesus and his message have no, or at least no decisive, significance for the Christian faith. . . . The problem of the historical Jesus is of recent origin; the date of its birth can be precisely fixed at 1778. That date tells us that the problem of the historical Jesus is a child of the Enlightenment.[1]

In the centuries prior to the Enlightenment, theologians were convinced that the Gospels give us absolutely reliable information about Jesus. They recognized the historical basis of the kerygma and saw no particular problem in that position. During the two centuries prior to the Enlightenment, New Testament studies of the Gospels were largely concerned with paraphrasing and harmonizing the four Gospels. New Testament exegesis was looked upon as a handmaid

1. Trans. Norman Perrin (Philadelphia: Fortress, 1964), pp. 1–3.

to the study of dogmatics. Essentially the same perspective was expressed by the late J. Gresham Machen of Princeton and Westminster seminaries: "For my part, I have always regarded the study of the New Testament, to which I have given my life, as ancillary to that other department [i.e., systematic theology]. New Testament study has its own methods, indeed; but ultimately its aim should be to aid in the establishment of that system of doctrine that the Scriptures contain."[2] And I was surprised to find a similar view expressed by Reginald Fuller, a New Testament scholar now at Virginia Theological Seminary. Such views are quite rare since the Enlightenment and the Old Quest for the historical Jesus. This has led frequently to a conflict between departments and disciplines and faculties. Unfortunately the influence is sometimes found within evangelical schools as well today. This type of conflict between dogmatics and other theological disciplines is unwarranted, unhealthy, and it reflects foreign theological influences. The Old Quest deliberately made such a contrast between historical and dogmatic studies, and it did so for principial reasons.

The Enlightenment and the Old Quest

The Old Quest of the historical Jesus was a product of the Enlightenment, as we have seen. And what was the Enlightenment? The Enlightenment was that early-eighteenth-century movement which tried to secularize every department of human life and thought. It was a revolt not only against the power of the institutional church but also against religion as such. The Enlightenment forces appear to be especially powerful in our own day as secularism advances.

The philosophical presuppositions of the Enlightenment were those of the rationalism of Descartes, Spinoza, and Leibniz on the one hand and the empiricism of Locke, Berkeley, and Hume on the other. These two opposing strands of thought were somewhat miraculously woven together by Kant, the great philosopher of the Enlightenment. Kant, who lived from 1724 to 1804, distinguished the noumenal

2. In *Contemporary American Theology*, ed. Vergilius Ferm (Chicago: Round Table, 1932), p. 253. Cf. Fred H. Klooster, *The Adjective in "Systematic Theology"* (Grand Rapids: Calvin Theological Seminary, 1963).

realm from the phenomenal realm and the practical reason (faith) from the pure reason. This Kantian distinction is basic for most of modern thought, and it is crucial for the subject of faith and history today. I reject Kant's distinctions, but I contend that his perspective is basic for understanding the developments of modern theology with respect to the question of the historical Jesus.

According to Kant the noumenal realm is the realm of God, freedom, and immortality. Only the practical reason or faith has access to this noumenal realm. The phenomenal realm, on the other hand, is open to sense perception and is controlled by the pure reason. It is only with respect to this phenomenal realm that the sciences are concerned. Modern natural science, historical science, indeed, all the modern sciences are rooted in this Kantian distinction of the noumenal and phenomenal realms and the practical and the pure reason. The distinction made by some modern theologians between *Historie* and *Geschichte* also reflects this Kantian distinction, or rather, Kantian dichotomy.

The secularization of human thought and the secularization of modern science which flowed from the Enlightenment was also applied to theology. Presuppositions which excluded anything supernatural were at work in historical science as the quest for the historical Jesus began. The entire emphasis came to be upon history as a purely natural, cause-and-effect relationship. Divine revelation and divine activity in history were excluded a priori. Thus, with the tools of the modern historian, the question was asked: What really *happened?* What *really* happened? The historian, operating, it was supposed, without any presuppositions, would be able objectively to answer these questions. Take away the old dogmas of the church. Exclude the previous assertions of the church and theology. Examine Scripture as simply a human product. Put away all presuppositions, and with complete objectivity let the historian discover who Jesus really was. The objective historian will be able to tell us *"wie es eigentlich gewesen wäre."* As someone has expressed it, this idea of moving into history without any presuppositions is as innocent as assuming that historians are as neuter as eunuchs. History itself was to show how unwarranted those presuppositions were.

The first representatives of the Old Quest simply went to work as modern historians in search of the historical Jesus. During the nineteenth century Friedrich Schleiermacher and Albrecht Ritschl, both systematic theologians, attempted to make theology scientifically respectable in the light of Kantian philosophy. But the main problem had been posed by Gotthold Lessing: Can a contingent event of history have eternal significance? That question is a tremendously significant one, especially for the Christian! We ought not neglect it. We have no right to bypass it or consider it superficial. And I know of no way of responding to that question except in the response of faith! It is true that some events have eternal significance. The cross of Jesus Christ is such an event. What a tremendously significant event that was. Our eternal salvation is dependent upon this cross of Jesus Christ, "who was delivered for our offenses, and was raised again for our justification" (Rom. 4:25 AV). What significant events they were—incarnation, crucifixion, resurrection! And it all happened way back there in history, in Palestine, once for all! Anyone who comes with Enlightenment presuppositions—that is, with humanistic presuppositions—is bound to ask how any event way back there in that obscure land can have eternal significance. You see that he is asking a crucial question, one that gets at the very heart of the Christian claim. Lessing's question is really the question of the Old Quest, and his question persists throughout the subsequent quests as well.

Reimarus's Naturalistic View

The Old Quest of the historical Jesus began with Hermann Samuel Reimarus, who lived from 1694 to 1768. His major writings on this subject were circulated during his lifetime among his acquaintances as an anonymous manuscript, and fragments were published by Lessing from 1774 to 1778. They were called the *Wolfenbüttel Fragments*,[3] and hence the beginning of the Old Quest is usually dated in 1778.

Reimarus was the son of a scholar who had studied the-

---

3. See *Reimarus: Fragments*, trans. R. S. Fraser (Philadelphia: Fortress, 1970).

ology and the grandson of a clergyman. He taught for a time in the philosophical faculty of the University of Wittenberg, but he spent most of his academic life as professor of oriental languages at the Hamburg Academic Gymnasium (1727–1768). A contemporary of Leibniz, Wolff, Locke, Berkeley, and Hume, Reimarus displays the strong influence of English Deism and Wolffian rationalism. When the *Wolfenbüttel Fragments* were first published, they created quite a stir; there was great agitation and strong opposition to the publication in general. When it became known that Reimarus was the author, his family disapproved of further publication for the sake of their own reputation, the safety of their possessions, and general family health. Students preparing for the ministry found themselves perplexed, and many turned to other professions.

Reimarus drove a wedge between Jesus and Christianity and left only a portrayal of a deistic image of Jesus, a Jesus conforming to natural religion. Let me give you just a taste of Reimarus's position. He took his starting point in an examination of the content of the preaching of Jesus. He concluded that an absolute distinction must be drawn between the intention and message of Jesus and that of the apostles. The message of Jesus is summarized in two phrases of identical meaning: "Repent, and believe the gospel" and "Repent, for the kingdom of heaven is at hand." Since Jesus did not explain or define these commands, He meant them to be understood in terms of the Jewish meanings. Jesus was a full Jew religiously. He did not aim to establish a new religion. His single aim was to reestablish Jewish national independence. In this sense He was Messiah—a Jewish political Messiah. He hoped to awaken the Jews to a popular political uprising which would sweep Him into office. Since the nation was the Son of God, His claim to be the Messiah involved only something "within the limits of humanity." An historical understanding of Jesus' teaching requires that one leave behind the ecclesiastical dogmas of a metaphysical divine sonship and the Trinity and similar dogmatic conceptions.

However, Jesus' intention to awaken the Jews to declare Him their earthly Messiah and win a speedy earthly deliverance did not materialize. He waited in vain for the popular uprising. Jerusalem refused to rise. Thus Jesus' life ended in tragedy. Before His arrest He was overwhelmed with dread, and His cry of despair from the cross—"My God! my God! why hast Thou forsaken me?"—indicates the complete failure of His mission. The Jews had not responded, and God had failed Him.

According to Reimarus, the aims and intentions of the disciples then came into the foreground. Initially there was a period of gloom. They had no resources of their own. During the three years of following Jesus, they had forgotten how to work. They did not desire to return to their old haunts. How were they now to support themselves? The only way they knew was by preaching. Reimarus regarded the resurrection narratives as contradictory. Besides, he contended, Jesus had never said a word to the disciples about dying and rising again. So Reimarus suggested a naturalistic view of the resurrection. The disciples stole the body of Jesus. They waited for fifty days to provide a cover-up. Then they invented the message of the resurrection, and they proclaimed the imminent return of Jesus as the Messiah. But the facts of history contradict the hope of a speedy second coming, and hence it cannot be true. Hence Christianity rests on a fraud.

This was the result of the first attempt to discover "who Jesus really was" by means of modern, objective, presuppositionless historical science. This was the way in which the Old Quest began.

Today it is generally recognized that Reimarus's answer was both absurd and amateurish. Jesus was not a political revolutionary, although that claim is being revived by some of the recent secular theologians. Most theologians today recognize that Reimarus did not do justice to the text of the New Testament. His deistic and rationalistic presuppositions created a new image of Jesus. Nevertheless, the Old Quest began with this attempt of Reimarus. The battle cry of the movement was "Back to Jesus, the man from Nazareth." Not Christological dogma but the personality and religion of Jesus Himself were to be decisive. The underlying assumption was that the Jesus of history and the Christ preached by the church are not the same. History and dogma are two different things. In this way the problem of the historical Jesus began.

Many others attempted to discover who Jesus really was. Numerous lives of Jesus were written during the period of the Old Quest. I shall not weary you with a rehearsal of all the types of answers. Schweitzer's book *The Quest of the Historical Jesus: A Critical Study of Its Progress from Reimarus to Wrede*[4] provides a comprehensive survey. I shall just mention H. E. J. Paulus and briefly survey the position of Strauss. Paulus, who died at Heidelberg at the age of ninety, showed Jesus as a morally exemplary man who taught the eternal truths of rational religion. He gave a largely naturalistic interpretation to the miracles of Jesus, the kind of interpretation that has become commonplace in liberal commentaries. The feeding of the five thousand, for example, was due to Jesus' starting a chain reaction in sharing His lunch. Thus there was more than enough to go around. There you have another instance of superficial interpretation presented in the name of historical science and genuine objectivity.

Strauss's Mythical View

David Friedrich Strauss represents the mythical approach to the Old Quest. By means of his mythical interpretation, he tried to break the deadlock between the naturalists and the supernaturalists. In some ways he is a forerunner of Rudolf Bultmann's demythologizing program. Strauss (1808–1874) died a century after the publication of the first of Reimarus's fragments. His famous *Leben Jesu* was published in 1835–1836 and went through several editions. By this time many lives of Jesus had been published, for the Old Quest had to fill in the gaps of the Gospels—especially with respect to the first thirty years of Jesus' life—in an attempt to explain how the child is father of the man. Strauss studied under F. C. Baur, was influenced by Schleiermacher's theology, and embraced Hegelian philosophy.

In the preface of his *Life of Jesus*, Strauss noted that supernaturalistic orthodoxy holds two basic assumptions: first, the Gospels contain history, and, second, this history

4. Trans. William Montgomery (New York: Macmillan, 1961).

is a supernatural history. Reimarus had contended that Christianity did not originate from a series of supernatural events but arose entirely from a natural set of circumstances; it was a fraud. Strauss agreed that Christianity was a natural rather than a supernatural development but disagreed with Reimarus on Christianity's fraudulent character. Strauss also disagreed with the rationalists of his day who, while rejecting the supernatural character of Gospel history, still maintained that the Gospels contain history, even though it is a natural history. But modern science, according to Strauss, could not rest satisfied with such halfway measures. The inquiry must proceed to ask whether in fact and, if so, to what extent, the Gospels are historical at all. He indicated that he did not feel adequately qualified for this further task, but he had not found anyone better qualified. Thus he concluded that the first assumption of the supernaturalists must also go. The rationalists or naturalists had not been critical enough. Historical inquiry requires that the Gospels be seen as mythical in character rather than as natural history. He contended that his mythical view sacrifices the historical reality of the Gospel narratives but retains their religious truth.

Strauss also stressed the Enlightenment objective of pure science without presuppositions. He did not want to avoid the seriousness of the scientific pursuit—objective and presuppositionless. He said that he had learned early from his philosophical studies to exercise that internal liberation of feelings and intellect from religious and dogmatical presuppositions. To the theologian who regards the absence of presuppositions to be un-Christian, Strauss replied that he regarded their believing presuppositions to be unscientific.

The introduction of the mythical consideration is the newness of Strauss's position in the Old Quest. As a left-wing Hegelian, Strauss emphasized ideas rather than events or personalities as the key to history. The seminal or creative force of history is idea. A person is usually necessary to bring the idea into history, but once it has been projected into history, the person or the originator of the idea is no longer essential. Parenthetically, we recognize that this is true of some ideas—Santa Claus, for example. We have all kinds of impersonators of Santa Claus, but the idea has been thrust into history without there (speaking from faith, you see) ever having really been an original real Santa Claus. Now according to Strauss, that is how we should look at Christianity.

Strauss contended that Jesus was there to bring the ideas of Christianity into history, but really it is only the ideas and not the person of Jesus which are the key to the Christian faith. Once these ideas have been projected into history, Jesus is Himself no longer essential to the message or the ideas. In this mythical motif of the Old Quest, the Christian faith can be explained without reference to Jesus Christ. Christianity is really an anonymous movement. One can see certain similarities here with Bultmann's position—with important differences, of course.

As a Hegelian, Strauss conceived the essence of Christianity as that of the union of God and man. Once this idea of the union of God and man has entered history, it no longer needs the original event to continue. The concept of the union of God and man entered historical consciousness through Jesus of Nazareth. But now that the idea has been projected into history, it no longer needs the person of Jesus or His history. Thus the mythical interpretation was Strauss's solution to his historical investigations. Historical studies led him to the conclusion that it is difficult to get at the historical life of Jesus because it became overlaid with myth. He doubted the reliability of all four Gospels. The effect of Strauss's work was to call into question the continuation of the quest for the historical Jesus. It was the suggestion of the Marcan hypothesis that opened the door to the continuation of the Old Quest. But according to Strauss the mythical form of the Gospels does express religious concepts or ideas. Thus even though the Gospels are unhistorical, their mythical form does have religious significance because of the ideas which they convey. And Christianity is basically the idea of the union of God and man. Here the kerygma has lost all historical foundation.

Diversity Within the Movement

After Strauss three general types appear in the Old Quest for the historical Jesus: the mythological, the liberal lives of Jesus, and the eschatological.[5] Although Strauss himself abandoned the mythical view and turned to a more liberal life of Christ in the second edition (1864), the mythical remained a basic type of approach in the Old Quest. As we just saw, this position reflects the influence of Hegel, according to whom the seminal creative force in history is *not historical personalities but ideas.* Thus Christianity is not the result of the life and work of Jesus of Nazareth, but of the idea of union of God and man. The mythical view did not gain many supporters after Strauss. The mythical thesis awaited Bultmann for further exploitation in the context of existentialism.

The second image of Christ emerging from the Old Quest is loosely called the liberal lives of Christ. In contrast to the mythical view of Strauss and the Hegelian emphasis, this group emphasized that history is made *not by ideas but by personalities.* Hence for these representatives, the major factor in explaining Christianity is the personality of Jesus. But as representatives of the Old Quest, they contended that the true personality of Jesus must be discovered by means of modern historical science. Anything supernatural or miraculous is discarded. Jesus must be understood as an ordinary human person—no matter how extraordinary or unique He appears. Thus the liberal school aims, on principle, to prove as unhistorical anything that is mysterious or supernatural in the life of Jesus. The image of Jesus that emerges is, as is typical of liberalism, that of a Socrates. The names of Albrecht Ritschl, Adolf von Harnack, Wilhelm Herrmann, and Ernst Troeltsch readily indicate the results of this approach in the Old Quest.

The third image of Christ that emerged from the Old Quest is that of the eschatological school. This school rejected the mythological and liberal positions because it saw in them dogmatic presuppositions which had led their proponents to read into the documents their own presuppositions. It was contended that an objective, factual reading of the sources leads one to see Jesus in an eschatological perspective. This school therefore regarded itself as the one

---

5. For this threefold classification and for some of the expressions used in this and the following summaries, I am indebted to Karl Adam, *The Christ of Faith* (New York: Pantheon, 1957), pp. 45–49.

that is truly faithful to historical inquiry. Representatives of this position are Wilhelm Bousset, Albert Schweitzer, Julius Wellhausen, and others. As Karl Adam expressed it: "With the help of a thorny textual criticism, they attempt to lay the original stones bare, and free them from all the secondary and tertiary strata. But indeed, pathetically little turns up by way of original stones."[6] It was soon recognized that the eschatological position was useful in calling attention to a neglected element but lacked authenticity in its exaggerated and one-sided emphasis. Something of the eschatological and apocalyptic is reappearing, again in different form, in the theologies of Wolfhart Pannenberg and Jürgen Moltmann.

We have seen that the Old Quest wanted to be objective and without presupposition in order to get back to the real Jesus, the Jesus of history. To do this, its advocates had to break with orthodoxy and free themselves from the dogma of the patristic and medieval and Reformation churches. The Enlightenment had brought about a shift from the dogmatic to the historical perspective. But the results were diverse and contradictory. Not only do the variety of types appear as sketched above, but within each type there is also wide diversity. As Jeremias summarized: "The rationalists pictured Jesus as a preacher of morality; the idealists as the ideal Man; the aesthetes extolled him as the master of words and the socialists as the friend of the poor and as the social reformer; while innumerable pseudo-scholars made of him a fictional character."[7] And he went on to say that "Jesus was modernized. These lives of Jesus are mere products of wishful thinking. . . . Dogma had been replaced by psychology and fantasy."[8] In a significant work on *History and Hermeneutics,* Carl Braaten presented this devastating summary of the Old Quest:

> The nineteenth-century biographers of Jesus were like plastic surgeons making over the face of their patient in their own image, or like an artist who paints himself in

6. Ibid., p. 48.
7. *The Historical Jesus,* p. 5.
8. Ibid., pp. 5–6.

the figures he creates. There was, in most cases, unmistakable resemblance between their portrayal of the religion of Jesus and their own personal religious stance. It also happened that the scholar usually found about as much as he was looking for. That is to say, he found out as much about Jesus, allegedly on purely historical grounds, as he needed to prop up his own theology. Nothing can make an onlooker so skeptical of New Testament scholarship as noting the frequency with which there occurs a convenient correspondence between what scholars claim to prove historically and what they need theologically.[9]

In this chapter I have bypassed Sören Kierkegaard (1813–1855), who lies chronologically in the middle of the period dominated by the Old Quest. But Kierkegaard did not really receive a hearing or make an impact until the time of Barth and neo-orthodoxy. Another important figure in this period to whom I have not referred is Martin Kähler, who published an important book in 1892 entitled *The So-Called Historical Jesus and the Historic-Biblical Christ*.[10] That title contains the two German words *Historie* and *Geschichte,* which have become rather significant in subsequent phases of this history. I shall refer to Kähler and Kierkegaard in the next chapter.

The Old Quest demonstrated the spirit of the Enlightenment and the beginnings of historical-critical science applied to theology. It is now evident that their claim to be objective and without presupposition was itself a myth. The Old Quest found only an ebionite Christ—that is, a merely human Jesus. His deity was denied by the presuppositions with which the quest set out. Jesus was regarded merely as a naturalistic or typical human being from whom everything divine and supernatural has been excised a priori. Thus the emphasis of the Old Quest on the historical ended in historicism—that is, a distorted history without kerygma.

The Old Quest set the stage and created the problems, and what has occurred subsequently is a see-saw effect from the Old Quest to the No Quest to the New Quest. Barth and Bultmann can hardly be understood except against the background of the Old Quest and liberalism. They sought

9. New Directions in Theology Today, vol. 2 (Philadelphia: Westminster, 1961), p. 55.
10. Trans. Carl Braaten (Philadelphia: Fortress, 1964).

to escape the impasse of those positions, and they ended with a view of the gospel hovering above history like a flying saucer which never really comes down into history.

A review of this history of the Old Quest provides an important lesson for us. There is an inevitable relationship between the Word and Christ, between Scripture and the Christ revealed in that Word. We see how the higher critical (Enlightenment) views which undermine the authority of Scripture are reflected in the Old Quest of the historical Jesus. When one loses faith in the authoritative, revelatory Word of God, the next step is also the loss of the authoritative Christ of the Word.

I think we can learn from the lessons of history and by the grace of God come to an even stronger conviction of the strategic interrelation of history and kerygma. Lessing did indeed pose a very important question. The Christian must in faith answer that question unhesitantly in the affirmative. Indeed, Jesus of Nazareth and the events concerning Him revealed in Scripture do have eternal significance. The gospel itself, the kerygma, is rooted in history —in Jesus Christ the incarnate Son of God who died on the cross for us on Good Friday and rose for our justification on Easter Sunday morning.

Chapter 2

The No Quest
and Neo-Orthodoxy

Let me begin with something of a parable. I took the plane
from Grand Rapids heading for St. Louis via Chicago. A
heavy snowstorm was moving into Grand Rapids; four
inches were predicted in two hours. Just as we were leav-
ing Grand Rapids, we were told that the plane was heading for Milwaukee instead of Chicago. From there I would
have to make new efforts to reach St. Louis. That struck
me as a kind of parable concerning the Old Quest. Representatives of the Old Quest wanted to try a new mode of
travel (historical science) to reach the historical Jesus,
Jesus as He "really was." They wanted to avoid the old
detours of church dogma. But after more than a century
of travel, they did not reach their destination. The historical Jesus could not be reached according to the travel
plans of the Old Quest.

New solutions and new modes of travel had to be de-
signed or discovered. Then Karl Barth and other neo-
orthodox theologians became the new travel agents. Barth
suggested, in effect, that if you want to travel to St. Louis
via Chicago but the plane takes you to Milwaukee, then
why bother traveling that way? Why not go *directly* to
St. Louis? Furthermore, there will be no trace of how you
got there; you simply arrive! There will be no vapor trails
in the sky, no tire tracks on the runway, no flight record,
no passenger list, no baggage check. You have arrived;
that is the only important matter. This is Barth's solution
to the problem of the historical Jesus. Now let me make
that a little more theological and concrete.

In some ways you might think that Rudolf Bultmann
would be a better illustration of the No Quest of neo-
orthodoxy. Yet Bultmann, in spite of his growing popularity
during recent decades, has not been of such foundational
significance for twentieth-century theology as Barth. Certainly Barth has been of far greater significance for systematic theology. Actually, Barth is more radical even than
Bultmann in terms of the relation of history and kerygma

—at least theoretically. Furthermore, I shall refer to Bultmann in the next chapter as background for describing the New Quest of the historical Jesus on the part of some of Bultmann's influential students.

Barth's Rejection of the Old Quest

Karl Barth lived from 1886 to 1968. I had the privilege of spending a sabbatical leave in Basel during 1959-1960. At that time Barth was lecturing on the last part of the *Church Dogmatics* that he was to publish—the fragment on baptism and the Lord's Supper. Barth died on 10 December 1968 while I was on sabbatical in Heidelberg. A few weeks earlier I had corresponded with him concerning the possibility of visiting one of his seminars again. In reply he indicated that his health had not permitted him to carry out his plans for a fall seminar, and he invited me to stop in for a visit when I did come to Basel again. He added that he would prefer that I come with some serious questions for discussion. That is the kind of man he was; even in old age and failing health he preferred serious theological discussion to mere socializing. Before I was able to make that visit, however, Barth passed away. Instead of a personal visit, I attended the memorial service held in the Basel cathedral on 14 December.

This giant of contemporary theology—that he certainly was—dominated the theological scene from the publication of his famous commentary on Romans in 1919. Although his immediate influence and popularity has declined in recent decades, his importance for twentieth-century theology remains intact. New theologies such as the death-of-God theology, secular theology, and revolutionary theology, as well as theologies of the future, are all expressed vis-a-vis Barth.

Barth's reaction to the Old Quest, which I tried to express figuratively or parabolically above, was expressed by him in his usually forthright manner. The skepticism to which the Old Quest led and the historicism with which it ended led Barth and his early circle of supporters to seek a new approach to the problem. It was really a new way of avoiding the problem posed by the Old Quest.

Barth and his early associates were skeptical of both

the aims and results of the Old Quest. As Carl Braaten expressed it:

> With one great shout the dialectical theologians—Barth, Brunner, Gogarten, Bultmann, and Tillich—disclaimed the historical Jesus. They took comfort in the saying of the apostle Paul, "Though we have known Christ after the flesh [*kata sarka*], yet now we know *him* no more" (II Cor. 5:16). This verse became the Biblical springboard of a theological triumph over the historical approach. The historical Jesus of the modern biographers is not the Jesus Christ whom the Bible presents; he is not the Christ of faith.[1]

Braaten continued:

> Karl Barth stated his conclusion in his usually explosive manner that the gigantic attempt of nineteenth-century "life of Jesus" research is not theologically worthy of consideration, whether it issues in the mildest conservatism or in the most imaginative hypercriticism; there is no good reason why historical research should go chasing the ghost of a historical Jesus in the vacuum behind the New Testament.[2]

According to Barth history can provide no basis for faith. Thus his conclusion is just about the exact reverse of the long quest for the historical Jesus which began with H. S. Reimarus.

In *The Historical Jesus* Heinz Zahrnt commented on Barth's reactionary stance to the Old Quest:

> "In history as such, there is nothing as far as the eye can see which can provide a basis for faith." This one single sentence dismisses the continuous, two-hundred-year-long struggle to make a tolerable basis for Christian faith in history, and establishes the infinite qualitative difference between God and man. God is God and man is man, and God is in heaven and man is on the earth. And man cannot in any way assure himself of the truth of God, even with the most exact historical method.[3]

1. *History and Hermeneutics*, New Directions in Theology Today, vol. 2 (Philadelphia: Westminster, 1961), pp. 58–59.

2. Ibid., p. 59; cf. Karl Barth, *Church Dogmatics*, trans. Geoffrey W. Bromiley et al., 4 vols. (Naperville, Ill.: Allenson, 1936–1969), 1 (part 1): 64–65.

3. Trans. J. S. Bowden (New York: Harper and Row, 1963), p. 68.

According to Barth, the Bible is really understood only at the stage at which the historical critic has finished his work. This does not mean that Barth rejected historical criticism in principle. On the contrary he contended that the critical historian must be even more radically critical. It is not what man thinks about God that really matters, but what God thinks about man. In one of his early essays in *The Word of God and the Word of Man,* he expressed it this way: "It is not the right human thoughts about God which form the content of the Bible, but the right divine thoughts about man."[4] In the preface to his commentary on Romans he said in a striking way: "But were I driven to choose between it [the historical-critical method of Biblical investigation] and the venerable doctrine of Inspiration, I should without hesitation adopt the latter, which has a broader, deeper, more important justification."[5] Yet he was convinced that he was not compelled to choose between the two. He clearly rejected that "venerable doctrine of inspiration" because he contended that it involves the freezing over of revelation. Nevertheless, he claimed that his entire energy in interpreting the Bible had been expended in the endeavor to see through and beyond history into the spirit of the Bible, which is the eternal Spirit.

Before continuing with Barth to show that his reaction to the Old Quest was so radical that he divorced the kerygma entirely from history, let us note some of the key statements of other representatives of the No Quest. Emil Brunner, like Barth, reacted to the Old Quest very sharply. In *The Mediator,* first published in 1927, Brunner stated:

> The question whether Jesus ever existed will always hover upon the margin of history as a possibility, in spite of the protests of the theologians, and of the Liberal theologians in particular. Even the bare fact of the existence of Christ as an historical person is not assured. It would be a good thing once for all to admit this consequence of (necessary) historical relativism. The question is only "solved" within the limits of historical evidence; this means, however, that the solution is not absolute. It be-

4. Trans. Douglas Horton (New York: Harper, 1957), p. 43.
5. *The Epistle to the Romans,* trans. E. C. Hoskyns, 6th ed. (New York: Oxford University, 1960), p. 1.

longs to the nature of the Christian religion to have such a Christ, whose historical existence can be doubted by nonbelievers, and even denied by them, without being able to offer any convincing proof of His historicity.[6]

Although Brunner's book was not translated into English until 1947, it was one of the early publications of the neo-orthodox position, and it expressed the strong reaction of the dialectical theologians to the Old Quest for the historical Jesus. Note again the key words in that quotation from Brunner—"Even the bare fact of the existence of Christ as an historical person is not assured."

Similar judgments were expressed by Paul Tillich and Rudolf Bultmann in those early years. Tillich's judgment is just as negative as that of Barth and Brunner. Recognizing the motives of the Old Quest as "religious and scientific at the same time," Tillich admitted that the "attempt was courageous, noble, and extremely significant in many respects. Its theological consequences are numerous and rather important." Then he added:

But seen in the light of its basic intention, the attempt of historical criticism to find the empirical truth about Jesus of Nazareth was a failure. The historical Jesus, namely, the Jesus behind the symbols of his reception as the Christ, not only did not appear but receded farther and farther with every new step.[7]

Bultmann also sounded the skeptical note in his book *Jesus and the Word* in 1926:

I do indeed think that we can now know almost nothing concerning the life and personality of Jesus, since the early Christian sources show no interest in either, are moreover fragmentary and often legendary; and other sources about Jesus do not exist. Except for the purely critical research, what has been written in the last hundred and fifty years on the life of Jesus, his personality and the development of his inner life, is fantastic and romantic.[8]

6. Trans. Olive Wyon (Philadelphia: Westminster, 1947), pp. 186–87.

7. *Systematic Theology*, 3 vols. (Chicago: University of Chicago, 1951–1963), 2:102.

8. Trans. L. P. Smith and E. H. Lantero (New York: Scribner's, 1958), p. 8.

What was it in all of these dialectical theologians that constituted the basis for this sharp reaction to liberalism and the Old Quest of the historical Jesus? I will concentrate on Barth in providing a clue to the answer.

Barth's Theology in General

As is well known, Barth's new theology developed as a response to the preacher's problem—Sunday's sermon. When he began his ministry in Geneva in 1909 and continued it in Safenwil in 1911, he was, by his own admission, a convinced liberal. He had been strongly influenced by Immanuel Kant's philosophy and by Adolf von Harnack and Wilhelm Herrmann, who had been his esteemed teachers. His Safenwil ministry spanned the years of the First World War, and during this period he became increasingly disillusioned with liberalism. With the bombs bursting on the nearby battlefields of Germany, it was difficult to retain faith in man, in man's inherent goodness and capacity to solve all his problems. Increasingly Barth sensed that liberalism did not have an authentic message for modern man, for a world at war. Barth was shocked when ninety-three respected German intellectuals, including some of his revered teachers, endorsed the Kaiser's war program. He concluded that a bad theology must lie behind such bad ethics. That sad day became a turning point for the young pastor of Safenwil. Gradually Barth, in company with Eduard Thurneysen, turned to "the strange new world" of Scripture and the writings of the Reformers.

Mainly it was the preacher's problem that led Barth to hammer out a new theological perspective. As he mounted the high pulpit each Sunday morning, he faced people eager to hear good news in the midst of world war. Perhaps it will help to understand Barth's problem if one can visualize the European pulpit and liturgy. In American worship services the organist usually controls the opening liturgy; the minister takes his seat, and after the organist has finished the prelude, the service begins, often with silent prayer or a hymn. But the European service is usually remarkably different. As the preacher mounts the high pulpit, the organist usually announces this event with climactic notes. It is a dramatic moment, one in which God's representative addresses the assembled congregation with the salutation—God's word of greeting. There is an atmosphere of expectancy as the organist makes way for the messenger of the Lord. I wish we could regain this dramatic moment in the liturgy in our churches today.

It was in that atmosphere, as he entered the pulpit each Sunday morning to face a people eager for the kerygmatic Word of the Lord, that Barth realized his liberal message did not meet reality. The optimism of liberalism did not conform to a world at war. The liberal message did not satisfy the needs and expectations of the congregation. It provided no comfort and joy and no realistic stimulus to the week ahead. At least Barth had the honesty to acknowledge that something was radically wrong. And what he said and wrote proved to parallel the life-experience of many other pastors and preachers.

It was hardly the way in which Barth spoke and wrote that gained him a hearing. When you read those heavy writings, you are amazed that they received a hearing at all. Yet the time was ripe for this rejection of liberalism. The cultural situation proved the collapse of liberalism. Disenchantment was a common experience to a war-weary world, the liberal optimism of which had been shattered. And Barth proved to be the spokesman for what many were experiencing. You recall how Barth expressed his own surprise at the hearing he had received. He referred to it as a man climbing the bell tower in the darkness. As he stumbled on the stairs and grasped for a handhold, he inadvertently grabbed the bell rope and started ringing the bell. And that ringing bell brought out the village.

Although Barth's theology developed in response to the preacher's problem, it was a solid theological reaction. Barth had been well trained by some of the best theologians of the liberal tradition. In this connection it is interesting to note that Karl's father was a minister in the more conservative wing of the evangelical church of Switzerland. When Karl wanted to study with the great liberal theologians of Germany, his father tried to steer him to more conservative teachers. As has happened so often in subsequent history, they compromised, settling for some less radical theologians. When Karl's urge was to study with the influential liberal systematic theologian Wilhelm Herrmann, the compromise was to settle on the field of church history, apparently less dangerous, with Adolf von Harnack. But none of these safeguards proved effective. Earlier, at one of these safer places of study, Barth began reading Kant's philosophy, and as he later said, it gripped him to the very depth of his being. After a semester in Berlin with Harnack, Barth finally reached Marburg and studied under Herrmann. In Herrmann he found his mentor, and Barth became a thorough-going liberal. The quality of his education and his own personal characteristics led him to provide a solidly theological response to his preacher's problem.

As he developed his new theological insights, Barth aimed to overcome the twin problems of liberalism—historical relativism and psychological subjectivism. These were also the twin problems of the Old Quest. They were looking for the historical Jesus, trying to discover who He really was and what He had really done, but the result was historical skepticism. The relativity of the Old-Quest biographies of Jesus was also clear. Every quester came up with his own subjective answers. Thus the corollary of historical relativism was psychological subjectivism, in which man is really his own creator and each man goes his own way. Here was the root problem that Barth tried to overcome.

In facing the problem, Barth introduced some significant changes from liberalism. He emphasized man's need of revelation and man's sinfulness in contrast to the humanistic Pelagianism of liberalism. But he introduced these and other changes by means of the distinction between *Historie* and *Geschichte,* a distinction that enabled him to keep the kerygma from being rooted in history. The price Barth was willing to pay to avoid historical relativism was to divorce the kerygma from history *(Historie).* Here the influence of the newly discovered Sören Kierkegaard (1813–1855) had its effect. With Kierkegaard Barth emphasized the *infinite, qualitative distinction between God and man, between eternity and time.* God is in heaven and man is on earth. A great gulf is fixed between them, and there is no way for man to bridge that gulf. The consequence of Barth's emphasis is that there is no revelation in ordinary history. The transcendence of God is Barth's emphasis over against the immanence of liberalism. And in this we see something of the Kantian dichotomy of the noumenal and phenomenal worlds again at work.

Barth's theological solution to his preacher's problem was to attempt a complete reversal of the liberal approach. As he liked to express it, he had to turn Friedrich Schleiermacher on his head. And that is what he did with the Old Quest as well. In place of the search for the historical Jesus, Barth declared, "No quest!" You will end up in Milwaukee instead of Chicago or St. Louis if you take that route. Go to St. Louis direct. That is the way Barth followed in terms of revelation and history.

Barth's View of Revelation

Proceeding from the Kierkegaardian emphasis upon the "infinite qualitative distinction between God and man, eternity and time," the emphasis upon the transcendence and freedom of God, Barth denied that there is or can be any direct revelation of God in history. In this way Barth denied any given revelation in creation and history (general revelation, or creation revelation); he also denied any special or redemptive revelation of God in history. Scripture is not itself God's revelation—it is *witness* to revelation but not revelation itself. If Scripture were itself revelation, God would be tied down to history; He would be "bound in morocco"; He would not be free; we would be threatened again by historical relativism. Barth went further than simply denying that Scripture is God's revelation. He also denied that there is a revelatory history (or salvation history) behind Scripture. Reformed theology acknowledges a progressive salvation history from Adam to Pentecost, but Barth denied a progressive salvation history. He denied that there is a series of historical covenants which God established with Noah, Abraham, Israel, etc. in progressively accomplished redemptive work in history. These negations should help in understanding his positive affirmations.

The only kind of revelation that Barth acknowledged is an encounter-event in the form of a theophany. For Barth there is only one (ever-recurring) revelation event and only one covenant (always the same). Revelation is that ever-recurring moment in which a man is directly confronted by God *sinkrecht von oben,* "straight down from above," the vertical touching the horizontal without entering it. It is like the tangent that touches the circle without coming into the circle. While the man to whom revelation comes is historical—a specific man at a given time and place in history—the revelation is never historical. This event of revelation, according to Barth, is the Christ-event. Revelation as the Christ-event is God breaking out of His hidden transcendence and confronting a given, particular man at a moment of time. That Christ-event is the pure presence of God confronting a man. And that revelation-event, the Christ-event, is always the same—God present to man. It allows for no history of revelation, no progressive unfolding.

This Christ-event revelation is not to be identified with Jesus of Nazareth. If Jesus of Nazareth were God incarnate in our history, then God would not be free. He would be tied to history and to history's relativities. That would bring us back to the old problems of liberalism and the Old Quest. One comes close to understanding Barth's position if he regards the inscripturated Jesus of Nazareth as illustrative of the Christ-event but not identical with it.

This is why I have tried to illustrate Barth's encounter-event with a flying saucer that hovers above the earth without really landing. That illustration may have some misleading implications as far as exposition of Barth's view is concerned, but it is useful as far as evaluation is concerned. I am thinking of the judgment that what looked like a flying saucer may actually have been nothing more than marsh gas. But as far as Barth's position is concerned, he was convinced that the event of revelation is a real revelation from God. It is not a subjectively induced experience. The experience is real, according to Barth, because God has brought it about. There is no way from man to God. And thus Barth tried to overcome psychological subjectivism by insisting that man in his immanence has no way at all to God in His transcendence. The price he paid for this safeguard is the denial of any direct revelation of God in history—no creation or general revelation, no Scripture revelation, no progressive, historical "salvation history," no series of covenants, in short, no revelation in history.

The technical form in which Barth set forth this concept

of revelation is that of the three-fold form of the Word of God—proclamation, Scripture, and revelation.[9] These are not three *modes* of revelation, but the threefold *form* of the Word of God. Revelation is always the Christ-event, a divine-human encounter, a theophanic event called "the Jesus Christ event." But this revelation-event usually takes place in connection with proclamation and Scripture. Proclamation (preaching) and Scripture are temporal, phenomenal entities of *Historie*. Everyone can see and hear proclamation and Scripture; they are historical *(historisch)*. But revelation is not *historisch;* it is *geschichtlich*. It occurs in the realm of the noumenal. When and where God pleases, this human, temporal, phenomenal, historical proclamation *becomes* the Word of God. That is *revelation!* That is the Christ-event! It is a noumenal event which the historian cannot touch. Only the immediate recipient of revelation hears and knows revelation. Beyond that he can only *witness* to revelation. Revelation is that noumenal *(geschichtliche)* event which happens when God sovereignly and unexpectedly chooses to use human proclamation based on Scripture and Himself speaks through it directly. And that event will always be something like the event on the Damascus road, which only Saul heard, not those traveling with him. It will be an event something like the burning-bush experience of Moses.

Barth's view of revelation has been designated *Christomonism*. That term highlights the fact that for Barth there is only one revelation-event—the Christ-event, the nonhistorical, theophanic, ever-recurring yet always-the-same, event of God's self-revelation. God's revelatory act, according to Barth, leaves no tracks, no footprints on the sands of time. Barth's view of revelation involves a theophanic happening with no historical *(historische)* tracks. It is like

9. *Church Dogmatics*, 1 (part 1) : 98–140. This is one of the most important sections for understanding the entire theology of Barth. In volume 4 (part 4, entitled *Fragments*), the lectures which I heard in Basel, Barth set forth a Zwinglian view of baptism and the Lord's Supper as the ethics of reconciliation. He no longer wanted to refer to these as "sacraments." The emphasis is not upon what God does in baptism and the Lord's Supper, but upon what man does in response to God's reconciliation. Hence the sacraments must no longer be considered part of proclamation as they were in volume 1. Volume 4 must be seen as a revision of the proclamation section in volume 1.

the flying saucer that was reported to have really been
seen, but did not land. It is like an arrival in St. Louis
without any trace of how one arrived and without any
general evidence that one was present.

Barth's View of History

The terms *Historie* and *Geschichte*, to which I have already referred, are very important to an accurate understanding of Barth's position. Unfortunately these German
terms do not lend themselves to accurate translation into
English. The problem is further complicated by Barth's brev-
ity in explaining these important terms. We have noted that
Martin Kähler introduced this distinction into the title of his
1892 publication *Der Sogenannte historische Jesus und der
geschichtliche, biblische Christus.* Bultmann and others also
employ the distinction, but there is no uniformity of meaning and usage in contemporary theology, and one must attempt to determine the precise meaning of these terms in
the context of each theologian's writings.

Initially Barth did not use the terms *Historie* and *Geschichte.* The first time this distinction between two kinds
of history appears in *Church Dogmatics,* he used the terms
general history and *special history.* His discussion of this
distinction at this place is actually one of the most detailed
anywhere.[10] Later the terms *Historie* and *Geschichte* appear
regularly in the sense of "general history" and "special
history," respectively.

By *Historie* Barth meant ordinary history, the kind that
everyone experiences and that historians (historiographers)
recognize and describe. *Historie* involves events which the
ordinary historian, the neutral observer (it is claimed),
acknowledges and describes. But *Geschichte* for Barth involves the acts of God, the event of revelation. Such "events"
are not open to the historian as historian. These events
bear no analogy to other events and cannot be acknowledged
as events by neutral historians. Such a *geschichtliche* event
is "an event as a fact with no court of reference above it
by which it could be inspected as a fact and as this fact."[11]

10. Ibid., 1 (part 1) : 373–78.
11. Ibid., p. 378.

Such *geschichtliche* events happen to a specific man at a given time and place in history; in that sense Barth opposed Bultmann's view that Scripture is mythical in character. The historian as historian is able to deal with the history of the *recipients of revelation,* but he is unable to deal with the *event of revelation.* Strictly speaking, there is also no history of revelation.

Thus the *geschichtliche* event of revelation is not *historisch.* The historian as historian can deal with proclamation and Scripture because these are temporal, phenomenal entities. But he cannot deal with the revelation (Christ-event), for this is *geschichtlich,* a noumenal event. The historian as historian may be able to deal with the *form* of the revelation, but not with the *content* of the revelation—that is, the revelation-event itself, the theophanic self-manifestation of God. Barth even went so far as to say that if the historian as historian should responsibly conclude that a Biblical event described as a real event *never* actually happened, that would have no effect upon the *geschichtliche* character of the event so described.[12] The implications of this statement are so far-reaching that they lead me to say that, at least in theory, Barth was more radical than Bultmann. This indicates why his position in reaction to the Old Quest is no quest at all. This is Barth's striking solution to the historical relativism of liberalism. The event of revelation, the kerygma, is so totally released from history that any relativism is out of the question. But is not this docetic trend of the No Quest just as unsatisfactory, just as destructive of the Biblical gospel, as the Old Quest was? Fortunately Barth was not as skeptical of history as his theoretical statements indicate. Nevertheless, this is how far he went to try to avoid historical relativism and psychological subjectivism. He did indeed turn the Old Quest on its head, but that is not the solution to the problems.

It seems clear that Barth's distinction between *Historie* and *Geschichte* reflects the influence of the Kantian distinction between the phenomenal and noumenal realms and between the pure reason and the practical reason (faith). Barth accepted the Enlightenment perspective on neutral,

12. Ibid., p. 375.

presuppositionless, historical science—indeed of all science except theology. As a result, in Barth's view the only science that has anything to do with God, revelation, and faith is theology. All the other sciences he regarded as legitimately secular (neutral). In removing revelation from the realm of ordinary history (except for the recipients of revelation), Barth set forth a docetic view of revelation. More than a distinction between two kinds of history is involved here: Barth's view removes the fundamental, basic, historical character of the Christian faith. The Old Quest has been turned upside down; the result is a No Quest because history as such is, according to Barth's view, inconsequential for the kerygma.

Barth's View of Christ

In the space remaining it will be possible to give only a hasty sketch of Barth's Christology. This will at least illustrate the issues already considered. We should note at the outset that the problem which must be solved, according to Barth, is not first of all the problem of sin. Rather, it is man's finiteness. The Kierkegaard problematic remains definitive throughout Barth's theology, even though in his later stages he attempted to distance himself from Kierkegaard. It is the infinite, qualitative distinction between God and man. The gulf, a yawning abyss, is the gulf of the infinite and the finite. According to Barth, reconciliation was needed even apart from sin. Sin is an episode *(Zwischenfall)* which determines the kind of reconciliation needed, but reconciliation was needed even apart from sin. It should also be noted that Barth rejected the idea of a historical fall. There was no state of perfection, no golden era, from which man fell. Sin was present from the beginning. Thus the real problem with which Christology is concerned is the problem of man's finiteness in contrast to God's infinity and transcendence. This makes the problem of revelation basic for the whole of Barth's theology, and what he understood by *incarnation* is given more importance than the cross and resurrection.

Another important perspective to bear in mind in approaching Barth's Christology is that he did not consider it valid to distinguish between the person and the work of

Jesus. Jesus' being as the Christ *is* His work. Barth's view may be designated an "actualizing of the incarnation," an "actualizing of Christology." It is not possible to make this point clear in a few words, but Cornelius Van Til has emphasized this consideration in his various writings on Barth. We have already noted that for Barth the event of revelation is the Christ-event, and this bears on the point now referred to. Barth's modalistic view of the Trinity, which results from an analysis of the event of revelation, is of course detrimental to any Biblical Christology. The very being of Jesus Christ is, according to Barth, His work.

This leads to the question of the role of Jesus of Nazareth and the significance of the years 1–30. Barth did not regard the historical Jesus of Nazareth as God in human flesh. That would go contrary to all of His basic views on the relation of God to the world and on the very nature of revelation. If Jesus of Nazareth were the revelation of God, then God would be tied to history and would not be free. Then the gulf between the finite and the infinite would be permanently bridged. That would be contrary to Barth's fundamental position.

The following complex quotation from Barth speaks to the questions raised here:

> The fulfilled time is the time of the years 1–30. But it must not signify that the time of the years 1–30 is the fulfilled time. It must signify that revelation becomes history (G), but not that history (G) becomes revelation.... God is and remains the Subject. The moment another subject is intruded here, the moment it is made the form of an utterance about time as such (even if it were the time 1–30), or about history (G) as such, or about definite contents of history (G) as such (e.g., about the "historical [H] Jesus" as such), it loses its meaning, at all events the meaning that alone can be proper to it in view of the revelation attested in Holy Scripture.[13]

This quotation indicates how opposed Barth was to any identification of revelation or the kerygma with history.

Then what about Jesus of Nazareth? Was He Himself revelation? This is a sample of the way in which Barth answered the questions:

13. Ibid., 1 (part 2) : 58f.

Thousands may have seen and heard the Rabbi of Nazareth. But this historical (H) element was not revelation. Even the historical (H) element at the resurrection of Christ, the empty grave regarded as an element in this event, that might possibly be fixed, was certainly not revelation. This historical (H) element, like everything historical (H), is admittedly susceptible of an even highly trivial interpretation.[14]

Barth was not simply distinguishing here between the event of revelation or the person of Jesus and one's faith-response to Him. He was denying that Jesus of Nazareth is Himself God's direct revelation. Barth did not personally deny that Jesus lived, nor did he express any doubt as to Jesus' historical existence. However, Jesus of Nazareth is really only Biblically *illustrative* of the Christ-event, the *geschichtliche* event of God's theophanic presence with man. Jesus of Nazareth is not God incarnate. Jesus of Nazareth is *historisch;* the Christ of faith is *geschichtlich.*

What then about such events in Jesus' life as the virgin birth, the crucifixion, and the resurrection? How did Barth understand these? The virgin birth is a *saga*, according to Barth. Jesus of Nazareth was born in the ordinary way that all human beings are born. The saga of the virgin birth points to the divine initiative of grace and to human passiveness in grace. In this sense Barth contended that all Christians are virgin-born and the Biblical saga is a sign of such grace. It appears that Barth's view of the virgin birth has more similarity to the Reformed view of regeneration than it does to the classic understanding of Christ's conception by the Holy Spirit and of His birth from Mary, the virgin. Some evangelicals have been confused by Barth's affirmation of the virgin birth in contrast to Brunner's denial of it. But in terms of meaning, Barth is closer to Brunner on this subject than to the evangelical or Reformed view.

Barth did regard the crucifixion of Jesus as an historical event in the sense of *Historie*. But the crucifixion *as revelation* is *Geschichte*. As such the crucifixion indicates the consummation of the incarnation. It too is more illustrative than *crucial*. Barth rejected the Reformed view that hu-

14. Ibid., 1 (part 1) : 373.

miliation and exaltation are states of Christ successive in time. They are but aspects of the revelation-reconciliation work of God. Only God is humiliated, and only man is exalted, in that event. Thus Barth denied that there was a transition from wrath to grace in history as a result of Jesus Christ's bearing our sin on the cross and bearing the wrath of God on our behalf. The kerygma is not tied to history. Barth's answer to Gotthold Lessing's question is quite radically different from the Biblical and Reformed answer.

The resurrection of Jesus Christ, according to Barth, is a pure saga.[15] It is an event of *Geschichte*, then, in which the narrative form is that of a pure saga, one that is not at all mixed with *historische* elements. This resurrection saga represents the pure presence of God. The virgin-birth saga at one end and the resurrection saga at the other indicate the divine initiative and accomplishments in grace. Barth included in the resurrection the forty days of Christ's appearances. Together they form one event. Similarly he regarded the ascension, Pentecost, and the second coming as three forms of one happening. They are not chronologically successive events in the life of Jesus of Nazareth. Rather, they are revelational, *geschichtliche* events that point to the one single Christ-event. And the name *Jesus Christ* is for Barth the dialectical term *par excellence*. In this term the divine and the human are brought together dialectically in the way they are always present in every revelational event. God and man are dialectically together in the moment of revelation, and in that timeless moment the gulf between the infinite and the finite is bridged without the bridge becoming a part of history.

However brief this survey of the complex Christology of Karl Barth is, it at least indicates the seriousness of his No-Quest theology. In reaction to liberalism and the Old Quest, Barth set forth the major form of neo-orthodox theology, in which Christology is completely divorced from

---

15. For a fuller discussion see Fred H. Klooster, "Karl Barth's Doctrine of the Resurrection of Jesus Christ," *Westminster Theological Journal* 24 (1962) : 137–72. I have also set forth Barth's view of reconciliation more fully in *The Significance of Barth's Theology* (Grand Rapids: Baker, 1961).

ordinary history. Here the Christ of faith is completely divorced from the Jesus of history. Barth's theology is docetic—docetic in terms of revelation in history and of a kerygma rooted in history. Barth "solved" the problem of the historical Jesus as projected by the Old Quest by completely submerging the problem, by completely divorcing faith from history. But the solution did not satisfy for long. The unanswered question of neo-orthodox theology soon arose to provide impetus for the New Quest for the historical Jesus.

Chapter 3

The New Quest
and Neo-Liberalism

Someone has said rather ironically that "the historical Jesus
is in fashion again today." The pendulum has swung once
more in theology. The unsolved or ignored problems of one
generation have a way of reappearing in the next, and then
they often stand in center stage. The Old Quest tried to
submerge dogma by emphasizing history; the result was
a historicism which sacrificed the kerygma. The neo-
orthodox or dialectical theology succeeded in suppressing
history for a time, but dogma was no more able to overrun
history than history had been able to repress dogma. What
has come to be called the New Quest for the historical Jesus
is usually dated from an important address of Ernst Käsemann delivered in 1953 and published in 1954. Käsemann
represents a new perspective evident in some former students of Rudolf Bultmann who saw an inconsistency in
their famous teacher and who tried to meet that inconsistency by renewing historical research concerning the Jesus
of history. Since the New Quest is set against the background
of Bultmann's theology, it will be necessary to sketch the
relevant features of Bultmann's thought.

Bultmann's No-Quest Theology

First, let us take a backward look and relate Bultmann
to the Old Quest and the No Quest. We saw that the Old
Quest arose out of the presuppositions of the Enlightenment and tried by scientific historical investigation to discover who Jesus really was. The Old Quest ended with
an historicism without a kerygma. It was ebionitic with
respect to Christ. Then as the First World War brought
to an end the happy optimism of the liberal era, Karl Barth
became the champion of a new theology which arose out
of the minister's problem with Sunday's sermon. Barth
tried to escape the historical relativism and the psychological subjectivism of liberalism, as well as its humanism
and immanence. He reacted against Adolf von Harnack and
Wilhelm Herrmann, his liberal teachers, but Kantian per-

spectives concerning the distinction between the noumenal and phenomenal worlds continued to dominate his thinking, even though Sören Kierkegaard became a new source of inspiration. For the sake of a parallel label, I have called Barth's theology a No Quest. Bultmann is to be included here as well. Taking the two together, we see that the No Quest emphasized what might be called an existentialistic kerygma—the term is especially applicable to Bultmann—which has little or no grounding in history. The Barth-Bultmann theology dominated the scene from 1919 to 1954, though it was not without impact after that date. In terms of history, the No Quest was docetic for it devaluated the historical Jesus and divorced the kerygma from real history. The No Quest was definitely a direct reaction to the Old Quest. Now some of the questions which Barth and Bultmann ignored or suppressed have again come to the surface and given impetus to the New Quest.

Rudolf Bultmann was born in 1884 and died in 1976. He was predominantly a New Testament scholar, and he moved increasingly to the left of Barth. While Barth tried to free himself from the tentacles of Kierkegaard—though I do not believe his attempt was successful—Bultmann openly acknowledged his debt to Heidegger and existentialism. Bultmann and Heidegger were colleagues at Marburg for a number of years, and Bultmann contended that existentialistic philosophy arrived at basically the same insights via secular philosophy that the New Testament presents. Thus Bultmann attempted to set forth a self-conscious existentialistic theology. And this theology, like that of Barth, seeks to establish a kerygma that is independent of history. Bultmann shared with Barth the desire to escape the historical relativism of the Old Quest and liberalism.

In contrast to Barth, Bultmann contended that the message of the New Testament is set forth in mythical garb—the world view current in New Testament times. In the face of modern science, Bultmann contended no one can responsibly hold that ancient world view today. He showed just how modern he was in his illustrations referring to our use of the electric light bulb and the wireless radio transmitter. Therefore, he contended, we must *demythologize* the New Testament, peel off the meaningless husk of

the mythical in order to rescue the meaningful kernel, which
is the message or the kerygma. The mythical world view
of the Biblical writers involves a three-dimensional view
of the universe, said Bultmann. There is the world up-there
and another world down-there, and we live down-here in
between these two. Are we to understand this primarily in
the spatial sense? Many students I contact regard the spatial dimensions as the heart of what Bultmann was talk-
ing about. I am convinced, however, that something much
more important is involved than merely the spatial. It is
not so much the spatiality of a heaven above and an earth
below and an underworld that I hear Bultmann speaking
about. Much more important to that ancient world view
which Bultmann conceived as mythological is the conception that man's life on earth involves the interrelations of
a living God as well as a personal devil, of demons as well
as angels. That is the real issue involved in the "three-
decker universe" of Bultmann. He contended that modern
man—man faced by modern science and technology—can
no longer put up with a world view that involves man with
a living, acting, personal God and with Satan and real demons. Hence the need of *entmythologizerend Denken*. Rejection of the three-storied universe of heaven, earth, and
hell involves more than mythical spatial concerns; it concerns the very nature of God and man and Satan! What
remained after Bultmann recast the gospel, after demytholo-
gization, was an existentialistic perspective of a self-
conscious, psychologically well-adjusted, modern, secular
man. That is the heart of Bultmann's kerygma. Parenthetically, the scientific perspective which Bultmann labeled
modern is really that of positivistic, nineteenth-century science. It has already been outdated by contemporary scientific views influenced by, for example, Einstein's theory
of relativity. This is the danger to which theologians have
often fallen prey; by the time they attempt to apply the
modern *Zeitgeist* to theology, they are already a generation
behind. Contemporary scientists smile at what Bultmann
referred to as "modern science." Although Bultmann worked
with existentialistic categories, the spirit of the Enlightenment was very much operative in his theology.

The radical hiatus between history and faith takes an

existentialistic form in Bultmann's theology. In the preceding chapter we noted the historical skepticism reflected in Bultmann's statement that "we can now know almost nothing concerning the life and personality of Jesus. . . ."¹ While he wrote those words in 1926, Bultmann remained rather close to that position throughout the further development of his theology. Yet he spoke of the resurrection and the incarnation, after they had been demythologized, as "eschatological events" rather than as historical events. He saw the resurrection, for example, not as the resurrection of Jesus from the grave, but rather the rise of faith in the disciples. A bodily, physical resurrection from the dead is ruled out by Bultmann's "modern scientific" presuppositions. The great presupposition of nineteenth-century theologians was that a person in history could not at the same time be, in a metaphysical sense, both God and man. And the great presupposition of the twentieth century, largely under the influence of Bultmann, is that resurrections from the dead cannot happen! Positivistic science, with its unbreakable cause-and-effect relations and its "principle of analogy," underlies this assumption. In this way, by means of demythologizing, the resurrection becomes an eschatological event.

Consider Bultmann's view of the incarnation. The idea of God really coming down and becoming incarnate is part of the mythological world view of the times. According to Bultmann the incarnation is not a datable event of the past. Rather, it is an eschatological event of the present that occurs in the context of preaching. It is the rise to faith or responsible self-consciousness (existential self-awareness) that a person comes to in the context of preaching. In that way Bultmann demythologized the event of the incarnation. Although Bultmann interpreted the incarnation by means of demythologizing and existentialism, one readily sees certain similarities to the theology of D. F. Strauss, although Strauss's mythical view was influenced by Hegelianism. One should also observe a certain similarity to Barth's view of revelation. Barth also contended that every event of revelation is really the event of incarnation which occurs in the

1. *Jesus and the Word*, trans. L. P. Smith and E. H. Lantero (New York: Scribner's, 1958), p. 8.

event of proclamation (preaching). God bridges the gulf when the event of preaching becomes the event of revelation and God is personally present to a man. That is also for Barth the event of incarnation. But Barth did not arrive at this position by way of demythologizing, nor did he openly embrace existentialism.

Bultmann thus set forth an existentialistic kerygma that is largely independent of history. For Bultmann the preached Christ is the real Christ. He contended that the crucified and resurrected Christ encounters us in the word of preaching and never in any other way. Thus, according to Bultmann, it would surely be a mistake if any hearer wanted to inquire back into the historical origin of preaching, as if this could demonstrate its rightness. That attempt would mean that one wanted to establish faith in the Word of God by historical inquiry. Rather, the word of preaching encounters us here and now as the Word of God, over against which we cannot put the question of legitimation. This preached word simply asks us whether or not we will believe it. This is really the emphasis of Bultmann's existentialism. Thus in reaction to the Old Quest, Bultmann was skeptical about any historical base for the kerygma. On this score Barth and Bultmann are very similar. But Bultmann's students discovered a certain inconsistency in their master, and this has led to the New Quest. We must take note of that "glaring inconsistency" in Bultmann.

As we have noted, Bultmann contended that "we can now know almost nothing concerning the life and personality of Jesus. . . ." Later in the same book, *Jesus and the Word*, he indicated: "The subject of this book is, as I have said, not the life or the personality of Jesus, but only his teaching, his message. Little as we know of his life and personality, we know enough of his *message* to make for ourselves a consistent picture."[2] Thus Bultmann's emphasis is the message of Jesus, and that means that the historical Jesus is really not essential to the message. Notice here the similarity to Strauss, who introduced the mythical view into theological discussion and saw history as formed by ideas rather than personalities. In view of Bultmann's emphasis

2. Ibid., p. 12.

upon the message of Jesus rather than the person of Jesus, he has said that Jesus is simply one of the *presuppositions* of the gospel.[3]

In spite of all this, Bultmann repeatedly stated that the bare fact of Jesus' historicity and His death on the cross provide the necessary historical basis of the kerygma. This has been called the "glaring inconsistency of Bultmann." While the kerygma is not really rooted in history for Bultmann and while he was skeptical as to what can be known from history about Jesus, yet he needed the fact of Jesus' existence and death for the sake of his message. It is this inconsistency which his former students recognized, and that recognition opened the door to the New Quest for the historical Jesus.

Before turning to the development of the New Quest, it is necessary to point out that Bultmann himself evidently recognized more historical certainty concerning the historical Jesus than these early statements indicate. Some of this more recent recognition on his part probably stemmed from the influence of the representatives of the New Quest. But some of his statements preceded Käsemann's lecture of 1953. In a *Festschrift* for Paul Tillich, Bultmann stated that Jesus of Nazareth is essential to the kerygma: "The content of the message (kerygma) is thus an event, a historical fact, the appearance of Jesus of Nazareth, his birth, but at the same time his work, his death, and his resurrection. . . . Christian preaching is the communication of a historical fact, so that its communication is something more than mere communication."[4] According to this quotation, Jesus is the content of the kerygma. But in what sense? Carl Braaten summarized Bultmann's answer:

> . . . not in the sense of a bygone religious personality, a hero of faith, or model of morality. He is the kerygma's content as an eschatological occurrence, as God's saving act of grace for all mankind. The kerygma proclaims the eschatological event. This raises a problem. If the eschatological event is at the same time a historical fact, then what is the meaning of Bultmann's decree that faith is

3. *Theology of the New Testament*, trans. Kendrick Grobel, 2 vols. (New York: Scribner's, 1951–1955), 1:3.

4. *Religion and Culture*, ed. Walter Leibrecht (New York: Harper, 1959), p. 112.

disinterested in what lies behind the kerygma, that we cannot and must not penetrate beneath the kerygma to the historical Jesus?[5]

Debate continues as to how much historicity Bultmann actually recognized.[6] But this is not essential to the issue before us. It is at least clear that Bultmann maintained that the sheer facticity of Jesus of Nazareth and His cross are historically certain and are necessary presuppositions of the message of Jesus. This has been called "the glaring inconsistency" in Bultmann. Essentially he insisted that the kerygma is independent of history, and yet the fact of Jesus' existence and death is somehow basic to that message.

It is worth noting that this inconsistency on Bultmann's part makes Barth the more consistent representative of the No Quest. I understand Barth to say that historical proof that an event recorded in the Bible (even the fact of Jesus of Nazareth) did not really happen does not prevent the story from being "regarded in its special nature, i.e. as history between God and man." This is how Barth expressed his judgment:

> Again, the judgment in virtue of which a Biblical story (G) was *not* to be regarded with probability as "history" (H) in the sense of the general concept, but perhaps with probability in the sense of the general concept to be regarded *not* as "history"—this judgment is not necessarily the judgment of unbelief upon the Biblical witness: for such a judgment may be passed and the story yet be regarded in its special nature, i.e. as history between God and man. The question that decides the hearing or not hearing of the Bible story cannot be the question as to its general historicity: it can only be the question as to its special historicity.[7]

5. *History and Hermeneutics*, New Directions in Theology Today, vol. 2 (Philadelphia: Westminster, 1961), p. 63.

6. In a lecture at the 1954 Marburg reunion of Bultmann and his former students, Bultmann admitted the following to be historically reliable: (1) the birth of Jesus during the reign of Augustus; (2) the life of Jesus within the time of Herod; (3) the ministry of Jesus in Galilee, especially in the region of the Sea of Gennesaret; and (4) the death of Jesus under Pontius Pilate.

7. *Church Dogmatics*, trans. Geoffrey W. Bromiley et al., 4 vols. (Naperville, Ill.: Allenson, 1936–1969), 1 (part 1): 375. Note that Barth did not here use the terms *Historie* and *Geschichte* in sharp distinction, but rather the terms *general history* (H) and *special history* (G).

The judgment I am here expressing about Barth's radical-
ness runs contrary to that of many interpreters, especially
more conservative interpreters of Barth. I might add a
personal footnote here. During 1960 when I was on sabbatical in Basel, Käsemann gave his lecture on the beginnings of Christian theology for faculty and students in
Basel. The next day on the way to class, I met Barth and
he asked me what I thought about Käsemann's lecture. After
a few comments I turned the question and asked for his
judgment. The gist of Barth's response was that it was
terrible; nothing is left of the gospel in that kind of Bult-
mannianism. I mention this incident to indicate that I am
aware of Barth's negative judgment of Bultmann and the
New Quest. Barth certainly did not want to be linked to
Bultmann. When he said what he did about Käsemann's
lecture, he was also aware of my serious difficulties with
his own position. He knew that I found the gospel seriously
impaired in his theology. Perhaps I may be pardoned for
adding another personal illustration on this score.

Admission to Barth's seminars in 1959 was somewhat
competitive. The number of students seeking admission in
those years was high. One was admitted on the basis of
the number of semesters he had studied theology. Since
registrars and academic deans do not dominate the academic
scene in Europe as they do here, the selective process takes
place within the classroom at the first session. This was
Barth's seminar on the first ten chapters of Calvin's *Institutes,* and I was eager to be in it even though the Latin
text of the *Institutes* was employed in the German discussion. Barth asked if anyone had studied more than a
certain number of semesters. I was one who had, and when
he got to me, I had to state, like the other students, where
I had studied. When I mentioned Calvin Theological Seminary, Westminster Theological Seminary, and the Free University of Amsterdam, Barth looked aghast. With a stut-
tering *"Ach, Ach,"* he asked, "Are you coming here to
convert me?" My reply was a short *"Sehr gerne, Professor."*
But I must now confess that I do not believe I was successful.

In spite of our radical differences in theological conviction, I found my sabbatical in Basel a very profitable
experience. In a variety of courses, I had the privilege of

nine class-hours with Barth each week for an entire academic year. I must also add that he did not succeed in converting me to his theology.

Thus, when I link Barth to Bultmann in terms of the historical question, I am aware of his own disapproval. However, I am convinced that this link is required by the approach Barth took to the historical question. And as I have indicated, in terms of the theory of his approach to this question, Barth may even be the more radical of the two. He at least avoided the inconsistency which Bultmann's students discovered in their teacher. I might add that Wolfhart Pannenberg also sees Barth and Bultmann basically at one in their approaches to the historical question. I shall refer to that in the next chapter. It is interesting to note that a current Bultmann interpreter also said that, with respect to Paul in I Corinthians 15:5–8, "Barth out-Bultmanns Bultmann."[8] However, I must now survey the New Quest.

Rejection of the No and Old Quests

Bultmann's graduate students have held annual conferences or workshops. They call themselves "old Marburgers." At the conference in 1953, Käsemann lectured on "The Problem of the Historical Jesus," and the New Quest is usually dated from this lecture. Braaten said that this lecture "rolled away the stone that blocked the passageway behind the kerygma."[9] If Bultmann, however inconsistently, required the sheer facticity of Jesus and His cross as the historical anchor for the kerygma, then at least the quest for the historical Jesus could be pursued further. Possibly greater historical certainty as to what lay behind the kerygma might be discovered. According to Braaten a common concern of the New Questers is to reassert the constitutive significance of Jesus for Christian faith. They follow Käsemann's lead in arguing

that since something can be known about the historical Jesus, we must concern ourselves with working it out,

8. Andre Malet, *The Thought of Rudolf Bultmann*, trans. Richard Strachan (New York: Doubleday, 1971), p. 158.

9. *History and Hermeneutics*, p. 68.

if we do not wish ultimately to find ourselves committed to a mythological Lord. The crucial issue is identified in "the question as to the continuity of the gospel in the discontinuity of the times and the variation of the kerygma," i.e., whether the proclamation of the exalted Lord through the Church is in some kind of recognizable continuity with the preaching of the historical Jesus, and consequently whether the exalted Lord is in continuity with Jesus of Nazareth.[10]

That summary is taken from James M. Robinson, the American representative of the New Quest. His book entitled *A New Quest of the Historical Jesus* was published in 1959. In a little more than a hundred pages he provided a good introduction to the new movement.

The major representatives of the New Quest are German theologians who were pupils of Bultmann, and consequently most of them are professors of New Testament. This is also true of Robinson, who is on the faculty of the Southern California School of Theology at Claremont. As I mentioned above, the impetus for the New Quest came with Käsemann's 1953 lecture to the "old Marburgers" on "The Problem of the Historical Jesus," which was published in 1954. Käsemann is professor of New Testament at the University of Tübingen. At the University of Heidelberg, Günther Bornkamm is professor of New Testament and an important member of the new movement. In 1956 he published a book entitled *Jesus of Nazareth*. Thus far he is the only Bultmannian who has published a book with that title, and the very title indicates a new approach after the long dominance of the neo-orthodox, docetic theologies of Barth and Bultmann. Bultmann's publication of 1926 was simply entitled *Jesus*. The English translators gave it, with Bultmann's approval, a title truer to its contents—*Jesus and the Word*. But the original publication—witness the quotations from it above—might better have been called *The Message of Jesus*. Thus Bornkamm's book on *Jesus of Nazareth* indicates that the New Quest reflects a remarkable change in the theological climate.

The names of Ernst Fuchs and Gerhard Ebeling are often

_____

10. James M. Robinson, *A New Quest of the Historical Jesus* (London: SCM, 1959), pp. 12–13.

found together in recent years because of their contributions to the "New Hermeneutics." But they are likewise representatives of the New Quest. Fuchs, formerly of Berlin, is now teaching New Testament at the University of Marburg as the successor of Bultmann. Ebeling is a systematic theologian in the movement. He was Emil Brunner's successor at the University of Zurich but is now at the University of Tübingen. Other major representatives of the New Quest are Hans Conzelmann at the University of Göttingen and Erich Dinkler at the University of Bonn.

The general aim of the representatives of the New Quest is to seek a closer connection between the kerygma of the primitive church and the historical Jesus. They are convinced that kerygma and history are interpenetrating in the Gospels. They are convinced that one must assert the constitutive significance of Jesus for the Christian faith. They start from the recognition that Bultmann was inconsistent in that, while he regarded the mere fact of Jesus' existence and death as essential to the kerygma, yet he did not pursue the quest for the historical Jesus. They consider his historical skepticism to be in part a negative reaction to the Old Quest. Thus they react against and criticize Bultmann because the person of Jesus was for him only one of the various presuppositions of the message and theology of the New Testament. As Käsemann expressed it, for Bultmann "Christian faith is here being understood as faith in the exalted Lord, for which the Jesus of history as such is no longer considered of decisive importance."[11] Thus they want to overcome the inconsistency of Bultmann by taking up again the historical quest.

In turning to the historical quest, however, these post-Bultmannian scholars do not simply return to the aims and programs of the Old Quest. It is a New Quest that reflects the influence of the neo-orthodox reaction to the Old Quest and the neo-liberal reaction to neo-orthodoxy. A good summary of the differences between the New Quest and the Old Quest was given by Braaten:

They do not wish to fall back into the biographical ap-

11. "The Problem of the Historical Jesus," in *Essays on New Testament Themes*, trans. W. J. Montague (London: SCM, 1964), p. 16.

proach with its interest in chronology, topography, and psychology. There is no inclination to deny the kerygmatic quality of the New Testament sources or to repudiate the insights of form criticism concerning the development of the gospel traditions. We are assured that the new quest is not being undertaken to look for proofs or to verify the faith by historical science. What then is it all about? It seems that they hope to find certain features in Jesus' own message which disclose his uniqueness, which make him more than merely a Jewish rabbi or eschatological prophet. If Jesus were just one more in a long line of rabbis and prophets, what special relevance would he have for Christian faith?[12]

According to Robinson, the representatives of the New Quest regard the Old Quest as *impossible* and *illegitimate*.[13] Two reasons are basic to that conviction: the Old Questers looked upon the Gospels as modern historical sources; and they followed the methods and procedures of positivistic historiography. Those two ingredients of the Old Quest are regarded as invalid.

Today there is a general conviction that the Gospels are kerygmatic in character and not simply histories or biographies. And under the influence of existentialism, a new view of historiography has arisen which replaces the positivistic view. This new view of history on the part of representatives of the New Quest involves the recognition of the historicity of the self. Hence the nineteenth-century claim of complete scientific objectivity has been widely abandoned. Also the cause-and-effect syndrome which characterized positivistic science has been replaced with greater emphasis upon history as "centering in the profound intentions, stances, and concepts of existence held by persons in the past, as the well-springs of their outward actions."[14] The emphasis is not upon objectivity and brute facts as in positivism, but upon persons and their intentions. Thus Robinson can claim that the New Quest is based "upon new premises, procedures and objectives."[15] Briefly, that means the recognition of the kerygmatic character of the Gospels as

12. *History and Hermeneutics*, pp. 69–70.
13. *A New Quest*, pp. 26–47.
14. Ibid., p. 39.
15. Ibid., p. 10.

well as the rest of the New Testament and a new view of history and historiography derived from existentialism rather than from nineteenth-century positivism. The New Quest, said Robinson, "is decisively interested in historiography of the twentieth-century kind, for the *kerygma* consists in the meaning of a certain historical event, and thus coincides with the goal of modern historiography."[16] In the New Quest, according to Robinson, one seeks an encounter with the whole person, comparable to the totality of interpretation one has in the kerygma. Yet the totality of the person is not to be sought in terms of chronological and developmental continuity, which is not only unattainable but also in a different order of "wholeness" from that needed to draw a comparison with the kerygma. Rather, the whole person is reached through encounter with individual sayings and actions in which Jesus' intention and selfhood are latent.[17] The existentialistic influence is readily transparent in this description from Robinson, a representative of the movement he is describing.

In summary, the New Quest is *new*, that is, distinguished from the Old Quest, because it recognizes the Gospels as kerygmatic sources, not as objective historical documents, and because it works with a twentieth-century view of history and the self which has been heavily influenced by Heidegger's existentialism.

Diversity Within the Movement

It is time to have a look at some of the results of the New Quest. Has the New Quest reached conclusions which are more Biblical and more congenial to historic Christianity than those the Old or the No quests reached? There is one important consensus reached by representatives of the New Quest with respect to the resurrection, which we shall consider shortly. It is an ironical consensus and a distressing outcome of the New Quest, but I want to see it in the context of other results of the experiment.

Apart from a consensus on the resurrection, it is interesting to observe that the results of the New Quest are

16. Ibid., p. 90.
17. Ibid., pp. 14, 70.

almost as diverse as the results of the Old Quest were. Yet the diversity of the New Quest is more restricted than the diversity of the Old Quest; it is more of a diversity within a single type.

Käsemann discovers the root of the kerygma in Jesus' *message* as Bultmann did. His brief analysis of the authentic sayings of Jesus leads him to conclude that "in spite of the absence of messianic titles, Jesus' understanding of his existence can be deduced from his intentions revealed in his sayings."[18] Fuchs, on the other hand, concentrates upon Jesus' *conduct* as "the real context of his preaching." Fuchs's understanding of Jesus' work and person are derived from His *conduct* and its interpretation in the parables.[19] In *Jesus of Nazareth* Bornkamm concerns himself more with the *events* of Jesus' life and collects whatever general biographical information is available about Jesus into a personality sketch. "Here it is clear that Jesus' eschatological message, including his eschatological interpretation of his own conduct, has been continued in christological terms by the Easter faith and the Christian kerygma."[20] Conzelmann "has united these various lines of development into a unified view of Jesus' eschatology and his person, in which christology replaces chronology as the basic meaning of Jesus' message: the kingdom which Jesus proclaims is future, but the 'interim' is of no positive significance to him.... This is the common significance of various themes which when taken literally could be contradictory: the nearness of the kingdom, the suddenness of its coming, and Jesus himself as the last sign. None of this is meant by Jesus temporally, but only existentially."[21]

Ebeling and Fuchs, more than the other New Questers, have

> attached their inquiry into the historical Jesus to a specific theological program. Together they have worked out a hermeneutical theory [generally called "the new hermeneutics"] that hinges upon the concepts of language

18. Ibid., p. 70.
19. Ibid.
20. Ibid., pp. 16–18.
21. Ibid., p. 18.

and faith. The key to the continuity between the historical Jesus and the kerygmatic Christ is faith as a word-event. They are not interested in a factual, biographical account of the life of Jesus. Rather, they seek what came to expression in him. Ebeling uses the term *Wortgeschehen* (word-event) and Fuchs prefers *Sprachereignis* (language occurrence). For both of them, what uniquely came to expression in Jesus was *faith*. To believe in Jesus means to re-enact the decision of faith which Jesus originally made. Faith is not a partial act; it is the whole man in openness to the future, living in relation to other men and sharing in love of God.[22]

According to Ebeling, Jesus is "the witness to faith" or "the witness of faith" or "the source of faith" or "the basis of faith," but Jesus is *not* the *object* of faith. "Faith in Jesus" as a combination of terms "is shorthand for attaining a pure trust in the love of God."[23] This approach of Fuchs and Ebeling is the link between the New Quest and the New Hermeneutics which is getting so much attention today. A helpful introductory survey of the New Hermeneutics is provided by Alan Richardson in *Religion in Contemporary Debate.*[24]

This very brief summary indicates that there is significant diversity among representatives of the New Quest, even though there is unity in the existentialistic approach. They all approach the question of continuity between Jesus and the kerygma in a similar way, which indicates the influence of Bultmann and Heidegger. However, they move beyond Bultmann in seeking a greater historical foundation for the kerygma. "Thus they search for a kerygmatic point of departure in Jesus' faith, in his preaching, his attitude or behavior, his self-understanding, his idea of grace, of God's nearness, and what not."[25] That summary is also a summary of the diversity within the movement. Internal friction within the school is also developing. "In the process of going beyond their master, they have brought about internal frictions of such gravity that the school is dividing into factions.

---

22. Carl Braaten, *History and Hermeneutics*, p. 71.

23. Ibid.

24. (Philadelphia: Westminster, 1966), pp. 81–101 (esp. 91ff.).

25. Braaten, *History and Hermeneutics*, p. 73.

Ernst Käsemann has written essays critical of Ebeling and Fuchs; Hans Conzelmann has warned that the new quest may once again arouse the appetite of historical proofs of the faith."[26] And Bultmann himself, though not uninfluenced by his former students, warned against the danger of their return to the fleshpots of liberalism.

Consensus Concerning the Resurrection

We must now consider the relation of the New Quest to the resurrection. While all the New Questers realize the necessity of continuity between Jesus and the kerygma, they all bypass the resurrection of Jesus Christ as a historical event. The results of their renewed historical investigations lead them all to conclude that the resurrection was basic to the kerygma for the early Christians, but the New Questers share Bultmann's presupposition that resurrections do not happen. Hence this crucial finding concerning the resurrection plays no significant role in the theological perspective of the New Quest. This led Braaten to refer to "the irony of the form-critical consensus."[27]

The consensus of the New Quest is best summarized in the words of Conzelmann: "The resurrection was regarded by the primitive church as an event in time and space. . . . Of course it did not *reflect* on the relation between the historical and the suprahistorical. . . . However, as soon as reflection sets in, . . . it is evident that historical research cannot establish the facticity of the resurrection. It can only establish that men testified they had seen Jesus alive after his death."[28] In other words, the form-critical study of the Gospels led to the clear conclusion that the early church started out from faith in the risen Christ. The essential content of the kerygma was the resurrection of Jesus. And "here lies the irony of this consensus," Braaten stated. "Nonbiblical factors intervene to deroute the theologian on his way from exegesis to dogmatics, so that—as is not seldom the case today—theologians will make statements which even

26. Ibid.

27. Ibid., pp. 78ff.

28. In ibid., p. 77. Translated from Conzelmann's article "Jesus Christus," in *Die Religion in Geschichte und Gegenwart*, 3rd ed., 7 vols. (Tübingen: Mohr, 1957–1965), 3:619–54.

they will admit run counter to central New Testament affirmations."[29]

The representatives of the New Quest share Bultmann's presupposition that resurrections just cannot take place. But that is a presupposition formed by the influence of positivistic science. As Braaten put it, "The impotence of the form-critical consensus can be explained by the stranglehold that historicism and existentialism together have had on the process of forming theological statements."[30] While form criticism analyzed the forms of the tradition in terms of the practical purposes they served—kerygmatic, didactic, liturgical, political—"it withheld judgment on the questions of reality and truth." And this "methodological reserve of form criticism . . . played into the hands of positivistic historicism and existentialism."[31] Thus "the interaction of form criticism, positivistic historicism, and existentialist interpretation resulted in collapsing the Easter event into the Easter faith."[32] The resurrection, from this perspective, concerns not the rising of Jesus from the grave but the rise of faith on the part of the disciples.

Thus the resurrection of Jesus remains the great stumbling block for Bultmann and the New Quest. And again the unsolved problem of one theological generation becomes the starting point of the next.

29. *History and Hermeneutics*, p. 80.
30. Ibid., p. 81.
31. Ibid.
32. Ibid., p. 82.

Chapter 4
The Now Quest
of Pannenberg

I wish to consider now what I have called the Now Quest
of Wolfhart Pannenberg. In this book I began with the
Old Quest for the historical Jesus, which ended in a historicism without the kerygma and with an ebionitic Christology. In reaction to that Old Quest and liberalism there
developed within the context of the First World War the
neo-orthodox theology spearheaded by Karl Barth. Because
of this theology's attitude to the relation of history and
the kerygma—attempting to escape historical relativism and
psychological subjectivism—I have called it the No Quest
of neo-orthodoxy. Neo-orthodox theology was historically
docetic; whatever kerygma it proclaimed was divorced from
real history. Especially in Rudolf Bultmann this was simply
an existentialistic kerygma. In 1953 the New Quest for the
historical Jesus was launched by a number of prominent
former students of Bultmann who recognized "a glaring
inconsistency" in their mentor's theology, for he insisted
that at least the sheer facticity of Jesus and His cross were
necessary to ground the kerygma. Sharing most of Bultmann's presuppositions and working with two convictions
that clearly distinguished them from the Old Quest—the
Gospels were kerygmatic sources, not merely historical
sources, and history must be approached from an existentialistic rather than a positivistic direction—these former Bultmann students launched the New Quest for the historical
Jesus. But they all stumbled over the resurrection. "The
irony of the form-critical consensus" was the major impasse
of the New Quest. While their historical studies led them
to the unanimous conclusion that the resurrection was the
key event for the early Christians, they were unable to make
that conclusion operative in their own theologies. Sharing
with Bultmann the positivistic presupposition that resurrections cannot happen, the results of their historical studies
were short-circuited. Thus the problem of the resurrection
of Jesus as a real event in time and space was a problem that
the New Quest tried to suppress. That problem has now

emerged as the center of the new theology of Pannenberg. For that reason I label Pannenberg's theology the Now Quest. It has happened again. The suppressed or unanswered questions of one generation emerge as the key problems of the next. The pendulum has swung, especially in Germany, from the Old Quest and liberalism to the No Quest and neo-orthodoxy to the New Quest and neo-liberalism to the Now Quest and Pannenberg.

Pannenberg boldly asserts a new "theology of history" in contrast to the theologies of both Barth and Bultmann. The essay which catapulted him to international prominence was published in 1959, and some regarded it as the signal of the end of the Barth-Bultmann theological epoch. Notice how Pannenberg set himself against both Barth and Bultmann in his programmatic essay on "Redemptive Event and History":

> History is the most comprehensive horizon of Christian theology. All theological questions and answers are meaningful only within the framework of the history which God has with humanity and through humanity with his whole creation—the history moving toward a future still hidden from the world but already revealed in Jesus Christ. This presupposition of Christian theology must be defended today within theology itself on two sides: on the one side, against Bultmann and Gogarten's existential theology which dissolves history into the historicity of existence; on the other side, against the thesis, developed by Martin Kähler in the tradition of redemptive history, that the real content of faith is suprahistorical. This assumption of a suprahistorical kernel of history, which was actually present in Hofmann's delimitation of a theology of redemptive history *(Heilsgeschichte)* over against ordinary history *(Historie),* and which still lives today especially in the form of Barth's interpretation of the Incarnation as "pre-history" *(Urgeschichte),* necessarily depreciates real history just as does the reduction of history to historicity.[1]

Thus the consensus "that the resurrection is not an historical event" is being challenged by some of the more creative theologians of our day. "Perhaps the most significant turn of events in the last decade," according to Carl Braaten,

---

1. *Basic Questions in Theology,* trans. G. H. Kehm, 2 vols. (Philadelphia: Fortress, 1970–1971), 1:15.

"is the discovery of the resistibility of the resurrection material to all hypotheses that fail to reckon with its historicity."[2] Precisely the impasse of the New Quest regarding the resurrection of Jesus is now being faced. The resurrection itself is made the center and fulcrum of the "theology of history" set forth by Pannenberg and the Pannenberg Circle. Pannenberg is a systematic theologian who approaches theology as a historian, affirms the historicity of the resurrection, and builds his entire Christology upon the historical event of the resurrection.

Pannenberg's Life and Work

Perhaps I should begin by telling something about the life and work of Wolfhart Pannenberg. He was born in 1928 in Stettin, which was then in Germany but is now in Poland. As was true of most Germans of that time, he was baptized into the church but was not reared in a Christian atmosphere. His youth was spent largely outside the church. His father was a loyal civil servant, and Wolfhart himself participated patriotically as a teen-ager in the efforts to defend Germany during the last desperate days of the Third Reich. It was during his university studies after the Second World War that he moved through serious philosophical studies to an intellectual affirmation of the Christian faith. A sympathetic biographical sketch written by an American acquaintance of Pannenberg may be found in the first fifty pages of Pannenberg's *Theology and the Kingdom of God*.[3]

Pannenberg began his university studies in Berlin, and, as is characteristic of German students, he moved about to various universities to study personally with the most important professors in his fields. In 1948 he studied philosophy at Göttingen under Nicolai Hartmann. In 1950 he studied at Basel with Karl Barth and Karl Jaspers. In 1951 he transferred to Heidelberg for one of the most formative periods in his life, a period of seven years. He was attracted to Heidelberg because of the emphasis upon the historical disciplines. Here he studied with Hans von Campenhausen,

---

2. *History and Hermeneutics*, New Directions in Theology Today, vol. 2 (Philadelphia: Westminster, 1961), p. 77.

3. (Philadelphia: Westminster, 1969), pp. 9–50.

Gerhard von Rad, the philosopher Karl Löwith, as well as Peter Brunner, Edmund Schlink, and Günther Bornkamm. Here Pannenberg became a member of a group of graduate students who gathered weekly for study and discussion—a group now called the "Pannenberg Circle"—finished his doctoral work, wrote a *Habilitationsschrift* (a second dissertation necessary for entering a university teaching post in Germany), and began his academic career as a *Privat-Dozent*. He then moved to the Theologische Hochschule at Barmen-Wuppertal, where he was an associate of Jürgen Moltmann for a few years. From there he moved to the post of systematic theology at the University of Mainz and then to the University of Munich (1967). He was a guest professor in the United States during the spring term of 1963 (University of Chicago) and during 1966–1967 (Harvard University).

One can divide Pannenberg's theological development into three decades: it was developed in the Pannenberg Circle during the 1950s; it was made public through publications and teaching during the 1960s; and it is now being faced as an important theological alternative to the theologies of Barth and Bultmann in the 1970s. When Pannenberg came from the University of Basel to the University of Heidelberg in 1951, he was invited to join a group of four graduate students who had been meeting regularly for some time. The four original participants were engaged in doctoral projects in Old and New Testament studies. We are told that "all four were interested in exegetical-historical questions, all were followers of Bultmann, and all were more or less shaped by problems in hermeneutics."[4] Pannenberg, who was working in the area of systematic theology, enlarged the scope of the group's attention. Some years later a student of church history and a student in practical theology and social ethics were added to the group. Because he was the leading systematic theologian in the group and because systematic theology brings the results of the varied disciplines to a unified focus, the group came eventually to be known as the Pannenberg Circle. Like the "old Marburgers," the Pannenberg Circle has also con-

4. R. L. Wilken, "Who Is Wolfhart Pannenberg?" *Dialog* 4 (1965): 140.

tinued to hold regular workshops or conferences. The focus of their concern, like that of Pannenberg's 1959 programmatic essay, has been the question of the relationship between faith and history. Thus drawn together by new historical influences emanating from the University of Heidelberg and increasingly disillusioned with Barth and Bultmann, a new "theology of history" gradually emerged from this interdisciplinary team effort.

The members of the Pannenberg Circle now hold important university posts in the major universities of Germany. Rolf Rendtorff and Klaus Koch are Old Testament professors, the first at Heidelberg and the second at Hamburg. Ulrich Wilckens and Dietrich Rössler are professors of New Testament, the first at Berlin and the second at Tübingen, where Rössler also teaches practical theology. And Trutz Rendtorff, brother of Rolf, is professor of church history and systematic theology at the University of Münster.

Their doctoral dissertations and *Habilitationsschriften* have been mutually influential upon members of the Pannenberg Circle. Apart from these and Pannenberg's important 1959 essay on "Redemptive Event and History," most of the publications reflecting the new theology appeared during the 1960s. The first of these was very literally a team project. At their semiannual conference in October 1960, papers were presented on the subject of revelation. In 1961 these papers were published under the title *Offenbarung als Geschichte* and appeared in 1968 in English translation as *Revelation as History*.[5] Rolf Rendtorff has a chapter on "The Concept of Revelation in Ancient Israel," Wilckens presents a chapter on "The Understanding of Revelation Within the History of Primitive Christianity," while Trutz Rendtorff deals with "The Problem of Revelation in the Concept of the Church." Pannenberg is the editor of the symposium and pulls conclusions together in systematic terms in an introductory chapter and in the main chapter of the book, "Dogmatic Theses on the Doctrine of Revelation." This little book presents a major, new view of revelation which breaks with the neo-orthodox view of revelation as personal en-

5. Ed. Wolfhart Pannenberg et al., trans. David Granskou (New York: Macmillan, 1968).

counter. I will return to Pannenberg's theses on revelation shortly.

By all odds the most significant of Pannenberg's publications thus far is his Christology, which in English translation is entitled *Jesus—God and Man.*[6] This work, which was first published in 1964, has been called "the most significant book on Christology since Emil Brunner's *The Mediator* in the twenties."[7] A small work on anthropology has appeared—*What Is Man?*[8] During the years Pannenberg has produced a large number of solid articles published in a variety of journals. Three volumes of such essays have appeared in German as well as in English translation.[9] Four essays which had previously appeared in United States journals are published under the title *Theology and the Kingdom of God.*[10] *Spirit, Faith, and Church*[11] contains essays by Pannenberg together with contributions from Avery Dulles and Carl Braaten. In 1972 an English translation appeared of Pannenberg's *The Apostles' Creed in the Light of Today's Questions.*[12] This work provides a brief statement of Pannenberg's position on issues not yet covered in major publications. Other books and numerous articles have been published by Pannenberg as well as by other members of the Pannenberg Circle. But these publications by Pannenberg which have appeared in English indicate that the literature on the Now Quest is already large and multiplying rapidly. The importance of the Pannenberg theology is evident from the fact that one volume of the important series "New Frontiers in Theology," edited by James M. Robinson and John

6. Trans. L. L. Wilkins and Duane A. Priebe (Philadelphia: Westminster, 1968).

7. Ibid., the dustjacket.

8. Trans. Duane A. Priebe (Philadelphia: Fortress, 1970). See p. 149.

9. *Basic Questions in Theology,* 2 vols.; and *The Idea of God and Human Freedom* (Philadelphia: Westminster, 1973). The SCM edition of the latter is entitled *Basic Questions in Theology,* vol. 3.

10. (Philadelphia: Westminster, 1969).

11. (Philadelphia: Westminster, 1970). See pp. 13–31, 108–23.

12. Trans. Margaret Kohl (Philadelphia: Westminster, 1972). See p. 178.

B. Cobb, Jr., is devoted to Pannenberg. This volume, the third in the series, is entitled *Theology as History*.[13]

Pannenberg's Theology in General

I shall now present some of the main features of the new theology that have emerged from the Pannenberg Circle and especially from Pannenberg himself.[14] First, we should note that Pannenberg is demanding a complete rebuilding of Christian theology consistent with the modern consciousness of history and sound historiographical methods. He is not just suggesting some minor revisions of Barth and Bultmann, but he sees the need for a complete new building project. Pannenberg does theology as a historian employing a revised historical method, one differing in significant ways from the positivistic method employed by so many modern theologians. Observe simply that most modern theologians have declared that if the resurrection is an event, it cannot be allowed in terms of historical method. Pannenberg's revised historical method enables him to regard the resurrection as a real event of history, and he regards it as the cornerstone of his theological building.

Second, as he goes about that task, Pannenberg definitely rejects the nonhistorical approach of Barth and Bultmann. His theology is developed in reaction to the No Quest of neo-orthodoxy as well as to the impasse of the New Quest of neo-liberalism. From his perspective, Pannenberg sees Barth and Bultmann as basically agreed in their divorce of the kerygma from real history.

Third, Pannenberg also rejects the distinction between *Historie* and *Geschichte* employed by both Barth and Bultmann and many other contemporary theologians. I am convinced that we can applaud the rejection of this much-abused distinction, since in most instances the distinction really stems from the Kantian distinction between the noumenal and phenomenal realms and between the practical and the pure reason. As such the distinction is frequently the result of the Enlightenment effort to secularize a large section

13. (New York: Harper and Row, 1967).

14. I am dependent in this section on various articles; the precise references I can no longer retrieve.

of life, the phenomenal realm. According to Pannenberg the distinction between *Historie* and *Geschichte* led many theologians to seek refuge against the storms of historical criticism by making faith its own ground, thereby exposing itself to the suspicion that it rests on sheer willfulness or illusion. Those are pretty harsh words coming from a modern German theologian against Barth and Bultmann, but I believe that Pannenberg is basically right in that criticism.

Pannenberg is not only aiming for a "historical anchor for the kerygma." A fourth characteristic of Pannenberg's theology is his emphasis upon universal history as revelation of God. Here one sees the extreme counter-swing of the German theological pendulum. Not just some history, but universal history reveals God. Oscar Cullmann's emphasis upon salvation history *(Heilsgeschichte)* is termed an escape into "a *heilsgeschichtliche* ghetto" by Pannenberg. To posit a restricted area of sacred history over against a secular history is to retreat to the ghetto, according to Pannenberg. He regards the development of a theological concept of universal history as the most urgent task to which theology is called today. As he makes this attempt, Pannenberg indicates that he is aware of the failures of previous speculative philosophies of history such as Hegel's. There is also clear evidence that Pannenberg has himself been strongly influenced by Hegel, at least in part. However, he thinks that he has both the theological warrant and the theological corrective for Hegel's shortcomings in the fact that the end of history has been revealed in the resurrection of Jesus Christ in a proleptic way. It is Pannenberg's contention that in the resurrection of Jesus, the future that God purposed for Himself and His entire creation—namely, the revelation of Himself to all men as their omnipotent, freely loving Father—was actually achieved in history. The resurrection of Jesus seen against the background of the universal aim of God in dealing with Israel and culminating in the advent of Jesus forms the core of Pannenberg's concept of universal history.

Fifth, the emphasis upon universal history via Hegel also leads to a somewhat rationalistic emphasis in Pannenberg. The theology of Barth via the influence of Sören Kierkegaard had a decidedly irrationalistic character. Similarly,

Bultmann under the influence of Heidegger called for the existential decision of faith. Both of these approaches were in line with the No Quest approach to the relation of faith and history, history and kerygma. In contrast, Pannenberg emphasizes the rationality of history and its openness to all observers. However, this rational approach of Pannenberg is one which includes the concept of revelation and even leads to the acceptance of the resurrection as historical fact.

Finally, Pannenberg does not, however, return to an open acceptance of Scripture as the authoritative Word of God. He rejects that approach as "biblicistic." In line with all the liberal, neo-orthodox, and neo-liberal theologians, he accepts the critical approach to Scripture. He also emphasizes the need for reinterpreting the Christian faith in relation to contemporary modes of thought. Only by such means can a creative reinterpretation and understanding of the Christian faith occur today, he maintains. Pannenberg is a complex modern theologian. In contrast to what he labels "biblicism," he indicates that he prefers the open rationality of the Enlightenment.[15] This point is especially important for some evangelicals who might be misled by the fact that the resurrection is so important in Pannenberg's theology. Some early comments about Pannenberg's theology, one of them in *Christianity Today,* hailed Pannenberg's theology as a revival of evangelicalism. Nothing could be further from the truth if one bothers to read the small print as well as the headlines.

These six characteristics are not an exhaustive description of Pannenberg's new "theology of history," but they at least set forth certain characteristics which distinguish the Now Quest from the New and No quests. I shall now examine some of his "dogmatic theses on revelation."

Pannenberg's View of Revelation

In his introductory chapter in *Revelation as History,* Pannenberg tells us that he and his theological associates are submitting a reinterpretation of revelation as *indirect revelation* through *universal history.* Both of those terms are important. It is not a direct revelation but "an indirect self-

---

15. *Revelation as History,* p. 14.

revelation of God as a reflex of his activity in history" that they emphasize. And it is not a revelation in some ghetto area, but universal history that they want to stress. In both of these emphases the opponents are Barth and Bultmann especially.

Now let us examine some of the "dogmatic theses on the doctrine of revelation" that Pannenberg sets forth in chapter 4 of *Revelation as History*. The first thesis attacks Barth head-on: "The self-revelation of God in the biblical witnesses is not of a direct type in the sense of theophany, but is indirect and brought about by means of the historical acts of God."[16] Pannenberg's point is that according to Barth, revelation is always a direct theophany in which God encounters a man in such a way that He leaves no tracks and makes no footprints on the sands of time. For Barth revelation is always a direct theophany outside of ordinary history. It is an event of *Geschichte* which the historian cannot touch. For Pannenberg, on the contrary, revelation is indirect, and it comes about by means of the historical acts of God. In this sense Pannenberg links up in a way with the emphasis of G. Ernest Wright on "the God who acts," although that emphasis went to an extreme. James Barr reacted vigorously to the one-sidedness of that emphasis because it failed to do justice to large tracts of the Old Testament, especially the wisdom literature. God not only acts but also speaks. Revelation according to Scripture is both a word and act revelation. Pannenberg also tends to undervalue the "word" of revelation in his overreaction to Barth's exclusively theophanic word-event. In this connection Pannenberg's historical-event revelation is also in opposition to the word-event or language-event of Gerhard Ebeling and Ernst Fuchs, although he makes no direct reference to them in his exposition of the first thesis.

Pannenberg's second thesis is: "Revelation is not comprehended completely in the beginning, but at the end of the revealing history."[17] Here Pannenberg approaches the idea of progressive revelation. Each historical event of revelation is not complete in itself, in contrast to Barth's view

16. Ibid., p. 125.
17. Ibid., p. 131.

of the theophany-encounter. According to Pannenberg, full and complete revelation, the *self*-revelation of God, takes place only at the end of the revealing history. This contention is inherent in the view that revelation is always *indirect* revelation. Indirect revelation through history involves a series of occurrences rather than a single revelatory event. Consequently God is fully revealed only at the conclusion of the series of events of history. There is an eschatology to revelation. There is a strong measure of truth in this thesis. The Old Testament looks forward to its fulfillment in the New Testament. And the New Testament, while rooted in the Old, also looks forward to the *eschaton* and the second coming of Christ when the *telos* will finally be reached. However, more than this is involved in Pannenberg's perspective. This will become clearer when we reach his thesis on the resurrection and its proleptic function.

The third thesis, regarded by some as the most provocative, is: "In distinction from special manifestations of the deity, the historical revelation is open to anyone who has eyes to see. It has a universal character."[18] Revelation does not occur in a ghetto, in *Geschichte*, in the noumenal realm. It does not occur privately in an I-thou encounter. It has a universal character. Hence it is "open to anyone who has eyes to see." It is historical and open to rational observation, not just to faith perception. Hence by means of historical investigation and rational observation, it can be known. It is here that Pannenberg would have been greatly helped by introducing distinctions that Calvin employed in the *Institutes*. The noetic effects of sin and the sinner's present inability to see and know the revelation that is clear and universal (the creation revelation), would have kept this thesis from its rationalistic overtones.

The fourth and fifth theses on revelation are also the heart of Pannenberg's Christology; they concern Jesus Christ and the resurrection. This is the fourth thesis: "The universal revelation of the deity of God is not yet realized in the history of Israel, but first in the fate of Jesus of Nazareth, insofar as the end of all events is anticipated in his fate."[19]

18. Ibid., p. 135.
19. Ibid., p. 139.

The term *fate* translates the German term *Geschick* and is used by Pannenberg with reference to that which happened to Jesus in distinction from that which He actively achieved.[20] Its primary reference here is to the resurrection, in which "the end is not only seen ahead of time, but is experienced by means of a foretaste. For, in him, the resurrection of the dead has already taken place, though to all other men this is still something yet to be experienced."[21] In other words, "the end of the world will be on a cosmic scale what has already happened in Jesus."[22] According to the fifth thesis, however, "the Christ event does not reveal the deity of the God of Israel as an isolated event, but rather insofar as it is a part of the history of God with Israel."[23] The event of the resurrection does not stand in isolation; it is the fulfillment of the "prophetic-apocalyptic expectation of the end."[24] When the people who had been formed by this prophetic-apocalyptic tradition heard of the resurrection of Jesus, they did not have to ask what it meant. Its meaning was immediately evident to them from this background. The end of the world had happened to one man. That is Pannenberg's understanding of its meaning. Unfortunately this makes the Christ-event, which for Pannenberg is the resurrection, illustrative of what will happen to all; it is not instrumental for what happens to believers. These ideas are worked out fully in *Jesus—God and Man.*

The sixth thesis concerns the use of Greek or non-Jewish terminology in the Christian mission to the Gentiles who did not have the Jewish apocalyptic background for understanding the event of Jesus' resurrection. I will not attempt an exposition of it now. In the final thesis Pannenberg is concerned with the relation of "word" and "event" in this new view of "revelation as history." The thesis is: "The word relates itself to revelation as foretelling, forthtelling, and report."[25] We have noted that Pannenberg rejects the

20. *Jesus—God and Man*, p. 32.
21. *Revelation as History*, p. 141.
22. Ibid., p. 142.
23. Ibid., p. 145.
24. Ibid., p. 146.
25. Ibid., p. 152.

Barthian view of revelation as "the Word of God" which is a theophany or direct *self*-revelation of God. He designates as gnostic the view of revelation in which "word" has eliminated history. However, events are not exclusive of words. There is an "authorized word" which accompanies the historical events in a threefold way: (1) word as prophecy, promise, or foretelling; (2) word as instruction, *didache*, or forthtelling; and (3) word as report, kerygma, or subsequent account. Thus the word precedes, accompanies, and follows upon the events.

We shall turn now to the main features of Pannenberg's Christology, in which some of these theses become more concrete and meaningful.

Pannenberg's View of Christ

The section of theology which Pannenberg has most fully developed thus far is his Christology. *Jesus—God and Man* is ambitious in scope and original in design. The key to his Christology is the resurrection of Jesus Christ, precisely the subject which constituted the impasse in the New Quest.

Pannenberg develops his Christology "from below." He starts out from the historical man, Jesus, and then moves to the question of His deity, and only at the end of the volume does he deal with the foundation stone upon which his entire Christology rests.

The late Jewish apocalyptic thought, specifically the expectation of a general resurrection at the end of the ages, is basic to his approach to the resurrection. In fact, this apocalyptic background is so basic to Pannenberg's theology that, to paraphrase Paul, if the apocalyptic is not true, then Pannenberg's theology is without foundation. Unfortunately we do not know very much about this apocalyptic as yet. Von Rad has said that we know virtually nothing about it. Both within and outside the Pannenberg Circle, increasing attention has been given to the apocalyptic materials recently.

As a historian Pannenberg analyzes the New Testament materials. He is especially impressed with I Corinthians 15, and the fact that Paul refers to many of the five-hundred witnesses of the resurrection as still alive makes this material especially interesting to the historian. There are two strands of evidence in the New Testament materials: one refers to the appearances of Jesus, the other to the empty tomb. Although Pannenberg regards the resurrection narratives in the Gospels as less satisfying historically than, for example, I Corinthians 15, he concludes as a historian that the resurrection must be regarded as an authentic historical fact. This is his firm historical conclusion even though, without telling us why, he states that the Gospel accounts do contain various legendary elements. In fact, he approaches the materials of the New Testament entirely as a critical scholar—using the tools of philology, textual criticism, form criticism, and the like. But he concludes that the only way to explain the rise of these two traditions— that of the appearances of Jesus and that of the empty tomb—is to recognize the resurrection of Jesus as a real event in time and space. Only if one has asserted in advance, by way of presupposition, that resurrections do not and cannot happen, can this conclusion be avoided. But, he contends, the historian as historian has no right to declare what can and cannot happen. It is his task to describe what has happened, no matter how extraordinary that event may be. Shortly I will summarize the new features in Pannenberg's approach to history which enable him to regard the resurrection as a real historical event.

Thus Pannenberg concludes that the rise of the resurrection traditions found in the New Testament are more plausibly explained by the hypothesis that Jesus rose from the dead than by any other hypothesis proposed so far. Therefore, he says, the resurrection of Jesus may be considered historically certain, that is, it is the most rational account of the available evidence and therefore something that every competent historian should accept.

In understanding what that resurrection means, Pannenberg uses as his model the postascension appearance of Jesus to Paul (Saul). He emphasizes the transformation feature of the resurrection of Jesus rather than the mere resuscitation of a corpse. Although Pannenberg's primary emphasis upon the transformed resurrection person is not necessarily in conflict with the Biblical view of the resurrection, his use as his model of the postascension appearance to Paul does make problematic a genuine physical, bodily resurrection. Transformation certainly demands emphasis, however, because Jesus' resurrection, in contrast to that of Lazarus and others, did not again issue in death.

The resurrection of Jesus, then, has retroactive significance—for Pannenberg, retroactive both ontically and noetically. The resurrection alone confirms Jesus' preresurrection claims to authority, and it establishes His divinity. Pannenberg's use of ontic retroactivity raises many questions for me. If he emphasized only a noetic retroactivity, I would have far less difficulty with his position. But it is apparently an existentialistic perspective according to which one "is what he becomes," in which "existence precedes essence," that he understands the ontic retroactivity. This leads to the question whether Jesus' divinity is really that of the second person of the Trinity, or a divinity which expresses the presence of God in Jesus analogous to God's presence in the Christian. I am increasingly impressed that any Christology "from below" has great difficulty in truly maintaining the unique divinity of the Son of God incarnate.

The resurrection of Jesus, regarded as a genuine historical event, is then the basis for Pannenberg's total Christology and, indeed, of his entire theology. However great the problems this theology raises for the Biblical Christian, the historical Jesus of Nazareth is basic to Pannenberg's view of the kerygma. And the resurrection of Jesus is basic to his view of the historical Jesus. Thus we do see a remarkable turn from the historically docetic theologies of Barth and Bultmann.

Unfortunately, when one examines what really happened on the cross of Christ, according to Pannenberg, and also what was really accomplished by the resurrection of Jesus, we find the results very disappointing. The Biblical pattern of atonement and salvation from sin is disappointingly absent in Pannenberg's theology in spite of the encouraging change of direction that this "theology as history" sets forth with respect to the relation of history and kerygma. But it is beyond the scope of this chapter to consider these issues further.

Pannenberg's View of History

Since the primary concern of this book is the relation of

the kerygma to history, I would like to set forth the main features of Pannenberg's approach which underlie his willingness to recognize the resurrection as an authentic historical event. This is certainly a new note in contemporary theology. It seemed as if the Enlightenment and the Kantian dichotomy of the noumenal and phenomenal worlds had forced modern theologians, other than the conservative, to deny that the historian as historian could legitimately deal with the resurrection. The contours of that perspective have permeated the positions considered in these chapters.

We have seen that ever since the Old Quest began during the Enlightenment, what came to be called "the positivistic view" of history and historiography dominated theological activity. Even the distinction between *Historie* and *Geschichte* in neo-orthodoxy continued to rest upon a positivistic view of history. From the side of German scholarship, Pannenberg is one of the first major theologians of whom I am aware, to challenge this positivistic view of history in significant ways. He rejects the evasion of history introduced by the *Historie-Geschichte* dichotomy. His comments on this important subject are all too brief. They are set within the context of his discussion of the question of the historicity of the resurrection. But the few brief statements constitute an important programmatic beginning, and some of his articles also add substance to the discussion. [26] The main features of his approach to history warrant a quick survey. In this position Pannenberg has been influenced by von Campenhausen of Heidelberg and many others, and his position has certain similarities to that of Jürgen Moltmann and Richard Niebuhr.

First, for Pannenberg historical reality is open to the activity of God; in fact, all of history is an indirect revelation of God, as we saw earlier. This acknowledgment involves a significant break with the positivistic, naturalistic view of history. It is a break with the Kantian distinction of the noumenal-phenomenal worlds. It is also a break with

---

26. See Fred H. Klooster, "Aspects of Historical Method in Pannenberg's Theology," in *Septuagesimo Anno: Theologische Opstellen Aangeboden Aan Prof. Dr. G. C. Berkouwer* (Kampen: Kok, 1973), pp. 112–27. See also Klooster, "Historical Method and the Resurrection in Pannenberg's Theology," *Calvin Theological Journal* 2 (1976): 5–33.

the *Historie-Geschichte* distinction of contemporary theology. Second, Pannenberg recognizes that all historiography is pursued by men with presuppositions, with a certain pre-understanding. It is important that these presuppositions not lead men to declare as impossible, events which have actually occurred. Pannenberg simply labels Bultmann's view that resurrections cannot happen a presupposition, and he rejects that presupposition. "If one assumes that the dead cannot rise, that any event of this type can never happen, the result will be such a strong prejudice against the truth of the early Christian message of Jesus' resurrection, that the more precise quality of the particular testimonies will not be taken into consideration in forming a general judgment."[27] "If the historian approaches his work with the conviction that 'the dead do not rise,' then it has already been decided that Jesus also has not risen (cf. I Cor. 15:16)."[28]

Third, Pannenberg contends that a correct view of history and natural law does not exclude the possibility of the resurrection. He rejects the well-nigh tyrannical power of the "principle of analogy" that has dominated the use of the historical-critical method. Pannenberg does not object to a limited and legitimate use of analogy. But he objects to the "omnipotence of analogy" by which Ernst Troeltsch meant "that all differences should be comprehended in a uniform, universal homogeneity."[29] Pannenberg opposes this in part by referring to more recent scientific views than those Bultmann appealed to as "modern." The following quotation deals with the issue as Pannenberg sees it:

> The possibility of the historicity of Jesus' resurrection has been opposed on the grounds that the resurrection of a dead person even in the sense of the resurrection to imperishable life would be an event that violates the laws of nature. Therefore, resurrection as a historical event is impossible. Yet it appears that from the perspective of the presuppositions of modern physics judgments must be made much more carefully. First, only a part of the laws of nature are ever known. Further, in a world that

27. "Did Jesus Really Rise from the Dead?" *Dialog* 4 (1965): 131.

28. *Jesus—God and Man*, p. 97.

29. *Basic Questions in Theology*, 1:46.

as a whole represents a singular, irreversible process, an individual event is never completely determined by natural laws. Conformity to law embraces only one aspect of what happens. From another perspective, everything that happens is contingent, and the validity of the laws of nature is itself contingent. Therefore, natural science expresses the general validity of the laws of nature but must at the same time declare its own inability to make definitive judgments about the possibility of an event's occurrence. The judgment about whether an event, however unfamiliar, has happened or not is in the final analysis a matter for the historian and cannot be prejudged by the knowledge of natural science.[30]

Of course not everything that Pannenberg says in that quotation can be endorsed, but the challenge to many still-current "scientific" claims is clear and valid.

Fourth, Pannenberg insists that fact and meaning are not to be separated. There are no brute facts; they always have a context of meaning. Pannenberg notes that "primitive Christianity did not make such a distinction between fact and meaning." Rather, "the occurrence and the meaning of Jesus' resurrection belong most closely together."[31] He rightly observes that the distinction between fact and meaning is "at home philosophically in Kantianism" and has "often been connected with the positivistic understanding of the historical method, according to which history establishes only 'facts'."[32] As we have seen above, the context of an event determining or giving its meaning is basic to Pannenberg's historical approach. That is why apocalyptic plays so important a role in his theology.

Finally, how does Pannenberg approach the question of "historical proof"? After examining the two strands of evidence for the resurrection of Jesus—the appearance tradition and the empty tomb tradition—he concludes that the resurrection of Jesus is the most probable explanation of the evidence: "If the appearance tradition and the grave tradition came into existence independently, then by their mutually complementing each other they let the assertion of the reality of Jesus' resurrection, in the sense explained

30. *Jesus—God and Man*, p. 98.
31. Ibid., p. 109.
32. Ibid.

above, appear as historically very probable, and that always means in historical inquiry that it is to be presupposed until contrary evidence appears."[33]

By means of these lines of approach, we see that Pannenberg at least partially breaks with the positivistic views of history and historiography. In this way he has rejected the presupposition that controlled Bultmann and contributed to the "irony of the form-critical consensus" and the impasse of the New Quest of the historical Jesus. Along the lines of the above considerations, Pannenberg at least concludes that the resurrection of Jesus is historically possible and must be accepted as a real historical event. In fact, as we have seen, it is an event of such great significance that his entire theology is built upon it.

33. Ibid., p. 105.

Conclusion

I have surveyed the long period of history since the Enlightenment of the eighteenth century and reviewed a number of very complex theological positions. The focus of attention was upon history and kerygma in relation to Jesus Christ. The Old Quest tried to discover who Jesus really was after faith in Scripture as God's authoritative Word had been relinquished. Their goal was to be achieved by means of the tools of modern historical scholarship. Thinking themselves to be truly objective and scientific, they actually embraced a new humanistic faith—faith in man. The "Jesus of history" who was "discovered"—"created" would be more accurate—was not the Jesus of Scripture. The "Jesus of history" set forth by the Old Quest and liberalism was not the Jesus of Scripture. Yet we must insist that Jesus of Nazareth is basic to the authentic Christian faith, basic to the kerygma.

Then the neo-orthodox theologians emphasized the importance of the kerygma while seeking to escape history. They discerned the historical relativism and psychological subjectivism of the Old Quest and liberalism, but their solution was an escape from ordinary history. In some this took the course of existentialism; in others the distinction between *Historie* and *Geschichte* had a similar effect. But this "kerygma" docetically divorced from history was not the Biblical kerygma. History without kerygma is not Biblical, but neither is a kerygma divorced from history. The Biblical faith involves an authentic kerygma rooted in what God has really done in history through Jesus Christ.

The representatives of the New Quest rightly recognized "a glaring inconsistency" in Rudolf Bultmann and set out again on a new historical quest. Thoroughly rooted in existentialism and sharing Bultmann's presupposition that resurrection from the dead cannot happen, the New Quest stumbled and fell on the historicity of the resurrection of Jesus Christ. The impasse of the New Quest was ironical because their historical studies led to the unanimous con-

85

clusion that the resurrection as genuine historical event was basic to the kerygma of the early church. The problem of history and kerygma remained.

Wolfhart Pannenberg has launched his new theology by recognizing the resurrection as the key historical event underlying the kerygma. In significant ways he has challenged the Enlightenment and positivistic views of history and historiography without fully abandoning them. However promising his Now Quest at first appears, he too has been unable to relate history and kerygma in satisfactory ways. The kerygma he presents upon the historical basis of Jesus and the resurrection lacks the authentic ring of the Biblical kerygma.

The Enlightenment perspective permeates all of the positions surveyed in varying degrees. The Enlightenment-faith reflects the crisis of the centuries, and the crisis of our own age as well, concerning Scripture and Christ. Who Jesus is and what He has done can only be truly known from God's trustworthy self-revelation, the authoritative Scripture. And it is by *faith* that we *know* this kerygma rooted in God's action in history. That is not to say that solid scholarly work is not needed by Christians; indeed it is. But scholarly work must proceed from Christian presuppositions and not from Enlightenment presuppositions. This is true of historical study as well as theological study. It is true of all scientific work. The Enlightenment crisis concerning Scripture also involves a crisis concerning Christ. The crisis concerning God's action in history leads inevitably to a crisis concerning the kerygma.

The various "quests" reflect man's autonomous attempts to create another faith and another avenue of certainty. The repeated failures and the repeated attempts at new ways to solve the old problems should be instructive for us. There is no substitute for the one way graciously opened by God Himself!

Index of Authors

BT
303.2
K66
1977

Klooster, Fred H.

Quests for the
historical Jesus

10482

DEMCO